STOP THE HATE FOR GOODNESS SAKE

How can classroom teachers disrupt discrimination and promote hope, foster healing, and inspire joyful learning?

Andrew B. Campbell

Larry Swartz

Pembroke Publishers Limited

Dedications

To classroom teachers and school administrators who are intentionally working every day in brave and loving ways to make our schools safer, more inclusive, and a place where our students and community can truly say, "I belong here." — A.C.

To Rachael Stein, a great teacher. Love, Uncle Larry — L.S.

© 2023 Pembroke Publishers
538 Hood Road
Markham, Ontario, Canada L3R 3K9
www.pembrokepublishers.com

Library and Archives Canada Cataloguing in Publication

Title: Stop the hate for goodness sake : how can classroom teachers disrupt discrimination and promote hope, foster healing, and inspire joyful learning? / Andrew B. Campbell, Larry Swartz.

Names: Campbell, Andrew B., author. | Swartz, Larry, author.

Identifiers: Canadiana (print) 20220177260 | Canadiana (ebook) 20220187207 | ISBN 9781551383583 (softcover) | ISBN 9781551389578 (PDF)

Subjects: LCSH: Social justice—Study and teaching. | LCSH: Multicultural education. | LCSH: Social justice and education. | LCSH: Intercultural communication in education. | LCSH: Race relations— Study and teaching. | LCSH: Anti-racism—Study and teaching.

Classification: LCC LC192.2 .C36 2022 | DDC 370.11/5—dc23

Editor: Kat Mototsune
Cover Design: John Zehethofer
Typesetting: Jay Tee Graphics Ltd.
Printed and bound in Canada
9 8 7 6 5 4 3 2 1

Contents

"Sometimes all you hear about is hate, but there is more love in this world than you could possibly imagine."
—from *The Boy, The Mole, The Fox and the Horse* by Charlie Mackesy

Introduction

"No one is born hating another person because of the color of his skin, or his background, or his religion. People must learn to hate, and if they can learn to hate, they can be taught to love, for love comes more naturally to the human heart than its opposite."
— Nelson Mandela (December 6, 2013)

Hate is a four-letter word. We might casually use the word *hate* to give a reaction or to voice an opinion of something. We might feel hate about something that we have viewed, read, or heard about. We might have encountered hate in news events, in fiction or nonfiction books we have read, in movies or TV shows we have seen. We might have been witnesses to hate in our neighborhoods, in our communities, in our schools. We, or someone we know, might have been victims of hate. Hate has always been part of our part of our personal, social, and political lives.

We might hate our peas or carrots, hate going outside in freezing weather, hate doing household chores, hate speaking in front of others, hate the sound of a mosquito buzzing in our ears, hate when technology fails us, or hate having to wake up early in the morning after a good night's sleep. There are many things that we may not like, that make us uncomfortable, angry, or afraid. But when we have a strong dislike or loathing for something, that is hate. When someone is hurt by the words or actions of others, that, too, is hate. And it needs to be confronted, disrupted, dealt with, and erased. To help prepare our students for some of life's challenges, it is important to take time to think about issues surrounding hate: *What are some things you hate to do? When was the last time you used the word* hate? *What does it feel like to be hated? What does hate sound like, feel like? What does hate look like? What can you do to stop the hate?* Our classrooms are places of teaching and learning, and it is vital that students be taught about hate. How can we help our students find answers to questions about hate, to raise questions about hate, and to think about what hate means to them as growing, caring citizens of the world?

How does hate come to us? Is it a feeling that lives inside waiting to crawl or roar out? Is it just a part of our emotional souls that sits alongside a batch of other feelings? The Rodgers and Hammerstein musical *South Pacific* is a story of racial prejudice, and when one characters asks, "Are we born with hate inside us?" another answers with the song "You've Got to Be Carefully Taught." The lyrics tell us that hate is something that is taught to us at a very young age, from the words, actions, and beliefs of our families, our neighbors, and citizens of the world who may be strangers to us. If we are to listen to the words of the classic song, it something taught from year to year, "drummed into" our ears until it is a part of our thinking.

Hate is the driving force behind anti-Black, anti-Asian, and anti-Indigenous racism, behind antisemitism, Islamophobia, Homophobia, Transphobia, and Cyberbullying. Consider the following scenarios: A Black youth knows he is being watched when shopping in the corner store; an Asian girl eating her lunch becomes upset when she notices other girls making fun of her food; a Trans girl is asked if she is a boy or a girl; a boy wearing a turban is mocked for being a "towelhead"; a twelve-year-old Syrian refugee with his uncle hears someone shout, "Go back to where you came from!" When we see hate messages scrawled on the walls of places of worship or hear someone make fun of our name, skin color, clothing, size, or place of birth, how does that make us feel? When hate is directed to us personally, or to someone we know or love, it can be a punch in the heart. We may then ask, *Why do some people hate other people? What would make someone so hateful that they intend to harm or even kill others?* and, most of all, *What can I do to make a difference?*

Hate on the Rise

"I am no longer accepting the things I cannot change. I am changing the things I cannot accept."
— Angela Davis, African-American political activist and scholar (McConnell, 2020)

Throughout the world, hate is on the rise. Recent reports from police inform us that nonviolent hate crimes have increased by 41% and violent hate crimes by 32% in Canada. Many of these crimes, according to Statistics Canada, were motivated by hate towards different races, ethnicities, sexual orientations, and other unchangeable aspects of identity. This information is critical for teachers to understand, as our students are affected by everything that happens outside of school as much as by events in school. To ensure that our students are protected, we must consistently find ways to disrupt, dismantle, and call out hate. However, many of our educators need better tools to effectively do so. In fact, the most common questions we receive at workshops are educator requests for resources about how to reduce and confront the rampant hate they encounter in schools and in the world. *Stop the Hate for Goodness Sake* was written with the intention of providing teachers with the necessary resources, information, and strategies to disrupt discrimination and to promote hope, foster healing, and inspire joyful learning.

As issues of hate remain prominent in the world, hate is also increasing within schools themselves. Recent surveys of Canadian youth tell us that more than half of racialized students had experienced racist comments or hateful name-calling at school, with many subjected to physical violence. As of this writing, stories abound: six Ottawa youth faced charges after physically assaulting and robbing a Syrian refugee classmate on his third day of school; multiple Toronto schools encountered smears of antisemitic graffiti (almost daily). One in four high-school students in the Ontario Greater Toronto Area have witnessed homophobic or transphobic comments or violence, while half of Canadian students have seen race-based bullying at school (Yuen, 2019; Fletcher, 2021).

It is no surprise that teachers and students alike need skills, resources, tools, and preparation to dismantle hate. To effectively confront and disrupt hate in schools, courageous conversations must be had so that braver spaces are fostered in classrooms, hallways, and the schoolyard. There are still schools and educational spaces that refuse to engage in these crucial conversations and to use the words *racism*, *white supremacy*, and *hate* to accurately identify the problem at hand. These are necessary and urgent conversations for all schools and all students at every grade level.

As we consider the preparation required to combat hate in schools, it is vital to recognize the power of disruption in education. Disruption involves taking intentional action to fight back against the societal norms that marginalize certain populations at the expense of others. These norms perpetuate hate and encourage inequity in schools and society alike. Disrupting these norms gives us the power to acknowledge and confront them, to actively choose love over hate. By leading with love and support for every one of our students, we will disrupt and dismantle hate in our schools.

In acknowledging the need for brave conversations, it is equally important to acknowledge the need for student voice. Students understand the experience of belonging, just as they recognize its absence. All students deserve the opportunity to have their voices heard and to share what they want their educational experience to look like. It is through listening to our students that meaningful change can be made (Campbell & Watson, 2021).

The timeliness of this book, alongside the rise of hate crimes and discrimination, offers teachers the tools they need to fight back against hate and lead with love. While hate may be on the rise, there remains hope that this hate can be disrupted and dismantled if we work together to cultivate empathy, interrupt normative attitudes of hate, and advocate for each one of our students in celebration of their diversity. Working inside and outside the lessons, gaining information, asking questions, and reflecting on stories, personal or fictional, can lead students to activism and to take action against injustice. We hope that this book helps teachers and students to make positive changes in their community and society so that it is more fair and just for everyone.

In this way, they will be doing their part to disrupt hate.

Why This Book?

The fact that you are holding this book in your hand validates the interest and concern on your part to help our students be taught about hate and to find a place in the crowded curriculum to deal with issues connected to hate and discrimination. We need to enrich communication skills, so students feel comfortable enough to share ideas and prod each other to think, question, explain, predict, wonder, and grow. We need to be committed to the goal of finding a place in our programs to provide contexts for talk and written reflection, where students share ideas and respond to what is offered by those around them. The 7 chapters and 28 lessons in this book provide a choice of strategies to reach that goal. To further this work, we need to create a non-competitive culture of listening and cooperation, and an ethic of hearing and valuing everyone's voice. In the book *Creating Caring Classrooms*, educator Kathy Gould Lundy (2011) writes:

> Some teachers might say they don't have time to do this: that it takes too much planning, energy, and time away from the real purpose of education— to teach the curriculum. It can be argued that creating a culture of caring *is* the curriculum.

Teaching students to respect one another, value differing opinions, share common experiences, and work towards a critical understanding of complex relationships and ideas is at least partly what school should be about. The goal of any inclusive pedagogy is to create learning environments that reflect, affirm, celebrate, and validate the diversity and complexity of the human experience.

Even if we all seem to have the word *hate* in our vocabulary, nobody wants to live in a society where people don't feel respected and included. Gathering information and reading stories can help us think about how we can be accepting, kind citizens in the classroom, in the community, in the world. *Stop the Hate for Goodness Sake* is designed to provide educators, families, and community members with a range of resources that provide information and strategies to encourage our students to open up their thoughts and feelings, and to better understand what they could do or say to stop the hate. Simply put, to stop the hate we need to

- Gain information
- Gather resources
- Introduce strategies that deepen understanding of social justice, diversity, and equity
- Be an ally and advocate, or an activist, and put your words into action

Hate is much more than turning our noses up at a vegetable we might not like. Hate is about put-downs, discrimination, and abusive verbal or physical action. Perhaps *Stop the Hate for Goodness Sake* can help adults and young people work together to come to a deeper understanding of the hate speech and hate crimes that exist throughout the world. More importantly, the active learning experiences—exploring definitions, participating in discussion, revealing our stories and listening to the stories of others, sharing our views and listening to the views of others, examining statistics, asking questions—are presented as a hub of ideas for teachers to bring this important work into the classroom. The information and lessons are intended to help you and your students think about your role in building equity and social justice for all. Perhaps students will see themselves in the content presented to them, making connections and raising questions about the challenges of stopping hate. Perhaps students will wonder about their own identity and the identity of others. Perhaps this resource will help contribute to understanding that all people of all races, abilities, cultural and religious beliefs, gender identifications and sexual preferences have the right to feel that they belong. *Hate* is a four-letter word. So is the word *love*. So is the word *kind*. And yes, for goodness sake, *good* is also a four-letter word. This book is offered as a source with the inherent belief that students had better consider all they can do to stop the hate, for goodness sake.

Throughout the book, lessons deal with some very sensitive issues, experiences, and language that might pose a trigger risk in the classroom. It is recommended that teachers use their knowledge of and relationship with their students to ensure that only lessons in which everyone can participate appropriately and safely are used.

Do all the good you can,
By all the means you can,
In all the ways you can,
In all the places you can,
At all the times you can,
To all the people you can,
As long as ever you can.

— John Wesley, cleric (1703–1791)

Acknowledgments

Our thanks and gratitude to

- Lindsay Cavanaugh, Ardavan Eizadirad, and Kaschka Watson for their commitment and passion to disrupt hate and promote social justice, diversity and equity. Heartfelt thanks for your written contributions #ISEEYOU
- Colleagues and educators who have contributed thoughtful perspective voice pieces and personal narratives to enrich the themes and issues of each chapter
- Mary Macchiusi for her wisdom and support
- Kat Mototsune for her sharp eye, wise insights, and scrupulous editing
- Dr. Karen Mock for her dedication to equity and ongoing commitment to conquering antisemitism
- Mrs. Stein's Grade 7 students for sharing their writing
- Margie Wolfe, who planted the seeds for this project

1

Defining Hate

Actions Define Hate

It is easy to click on social media and see news about a bombing, a hate crime, or anti-Black racism. Students live in a society bombarded by 24-hour news cycles, memes, a continual high online presence of social media, and increased awareness of the issue of hate. There is a debate as to whether hate-motivated incidents are increasing, or whether there is simply more documentation and capturing of hate.

Our students are developing into global adults and global citizens living in a multicultural society. To contextualize the hate they might encounter, here are a few of many examples of hate around the globe:

Country	Year	Description of Hate
Nigeria	2022	A mosque in Delta State is stormed by armed men and eleven worshippers are shot. The Muslim Rights Concern call security against the perpetrators, and the act is found to be a Muslim hate crime. (Adesina, 2022)
Australia	1980s to Present	In 2022, an investigation commences surrounding the four decades of unresolved deaths caused by gay hate crimes unknown to the police. (Mcguirk, 2022)

European Union	2022	Internet hate-speech crimes are committed in eleven European Union countries, most of which involve racism and xenophobia. They include intentions to commit offences against marginalized populations, hate speech, and direct calls to violence. (Europol, 2022)
Brazil	2020	Members of the Brazilian 2SLGBTQIA+ community are found to be disproportionately harassed and attacked because of their identity. As a result of hate crimes, more than 150 transgender people are killed in Brazil in 2020, representing the highest violence levels against transgender people in the world. (Francisco & Muggah, 2020)
United States	2022	A white shooter kills 10 Black shoppers and workers at a grocery store in Buffalo, New York, and pleads guilty to hate-motivated terrorism and murder in court. When the judge refers to each victim by name and asks if they were killed because of their race, the offender replies "yes" each time. (Craig, 2022)
United States	2016	49 people are shot at a gay nightclub in Orlando, Florida, in one of the deadliest mass shootings in the US. The gunman pledges allegiance to ISIS, making it the worst US terror attack since 9/11. (Ellis et al., 2016)
United States	2022	18 people are injured and 5 people killed by a gunman at a gay nightclub in Colorado. Two firearms are found at the scene after the shooting, resulting in charges of first-degree murder motivated by hate.
Canada	2022	Four Indigenous women in Winnipeg are honored by the community at a candlelight vigil after reports that they were murdered by a serial killer. (Rosen, 2022)

Canada	2021	Four Muslim family members are killed after a premeditated hate-motivated vehicle attack that leaves behind a nine-year-old boy as the family's sole survivor. (BBC, 2021)
United States	2018	Eleven people are killed after being shot in a Pittsburgh synagogue in a crime motivated by antisemitic hate. (Andone et al., 2018)
Jamaica	2013	A 16-year-old transgender teenager is killed after being stabbed, beaten, and shot by a mob of people for dressing publicly in drag. (The Associated Press, 2013)

Words to Define Hate

Clearly, there is a fundamental need for a reduction in hate. However, at the time of writing, the Government of Canada has yet to establish a clear and cohesive national definition for the term *hate crime*, making it challenging to collect accurate statistics on the subject and perpetuating the issue of inconsistent governmental and legal action against hate. The restrictive definitions used by law enforcement agencies have been found to cause disproportionate harm towards marginalized populations and to increase incidents of hate.

Simply put, a hate crime must include hate and crime. A hate crime is typically one involving violence that is motivated by prejudice on the basis of race, color, religion, national origin, sexual orientation, sexuality, gender, or gender identity.

Presenting students with an explanation of a hate crime is important so that they know and understand how hate can lead to criminal offences. With hate crimes, the word *hate* does not mean a general dislike or anger. In this context, *hate* means bias against people or groups of people with specific characteristics (defined by law) and according to federal law. Hate can be considered a crime when there is evidence of assault, murder, arson, or vandalism, or even threats to commit such crimes. Conspiring or asking another person to commit a crime, even if the crime is never carried out, can be considered a hate crime. Hate crimes, of course, affect families, communities, and, at times, entire nations.

A significant point that also needs to be made is that, even though there are thousands of hate crimes committed each year in every country, the majority of these are not reported to law enforcement. Reporting hate crimes is critical, not only to support and assist victims, but also to send a clear message that the community will not tolerate these crimes. Without reports of hate crimes, law enforcement agencies might not fully understand the scope of the problem in a community, thereby limiting the resources that could be put forth to prevent and address attacks based on bias and hate.

Lesson: Finding a Definition of Hate

This lesson outlines a series of learning events that has students think about the meaning of the word *hate*, and that invites students to work independently, as well as to collaborate with a partner, in small groups, and as a whole class, to write a dictionary definition of the word *hate*.

1. Introduce the lesson to students:

    A new dictionary is about to be published, but the word *hate* has yet to be defined. As expert dictionary editors, you have been called upon for input.

2. To begin, students work independently. Each student is given a file card on which to write a personal definition of the word *hate* as a noun and/or as a verb.
3. In pairs, students exchange definitions. Ask students to consider this question: *What word or phrases from your partner's definition do you think you might like to borrow to include in a definition of* hate? These suggestions can be recorded on a chart.
4. Pairs work together to synthesize definitions. Students are encouraged to include words from each partner's definition, as well as to add new words or phrases.
5. Partners are matched up with other pairs to share definitions. Groups of four collaborate to create a new definition. Challenge the students by insisting that the new definition be written in an exact number of words (e.g., 25 words). Once group definitions are completed, one member of each group shares the definition with the whole class.
6. The next phase is a shared writing activity. Students offer suggestions to create a class definition of the word *hate*. Record suggestions as offered, and revise and edit as the composing process unfolds.
7. After sharing dictionary definitions, have students consider which words from their personal definition are similar to or different from the definition found in a published or online dictionary.

A group of students in Grades 4–8 were invited to define the word hate.

Hate is…

… a feeling or something you can get mad at. *A.S., Grade 6*

… a word normally used with anger and negativity, jealousy and power. *L.S., Grade 6*

… when you have big negative feelings against someone or something. *S.S., Grade 5*

… hurting people in a rude way. *A.C., Grade 7*

… a strong dislike that can sometimes lead to violence or be a crime. *F.R., Grade 8*

… something that commonly results in pain and emotional hurt. *K.B., Grade 7*

… the act of disliking something to the point of wanting to see the destruction or suffering of it. *B.P, Grade 8*

… misunderstanding someone who is different from you. *T.S., Grade 7*

… a harsh word for something you don't like. *W.H., Grade 4*

… when you dislike someone so much that you don't even want to be close to them. *J.G., Grade 8*

… discriminating against certain people with different backgrounds than yours. *N.I., Grade 6*

… when you absolutely despise something or someone and you think that life would be better without that thing or person. *K.Y., Grade 8*

… something you feel when you don't love yourself. *M.H., Grade 7*

Out of 100 students who were asked to define hate, 75% used the word *dislike* in their definitions. Some used the words *really dislike*, *strong dislike*, *extreme dislike*, or *deep dislike*.

William W., Grade 7, defines hate by writing a letter to an imaginary alien creature

Dear Creature From Outer Space,

If you come to EARTH here is something you should know about our planet…HATE.

Hate? Sadly, we have it a lot here on Earth

Hate sounds like screaming police sirens, signaling yet another crime fueled by hate.

Hate feels like a headache, no matter how much water you drink, it is always there. Now matter how hard you fight against hate, there will always be haters.

Hate smells like smoke, thick and suffocating, trapping you like hate does and making you feel weak.

Hate travels like a fire. It can spread just as quickly.

Hate tastes like lemon, sour, and acidic replicating how it feels to experience hatred.

Do you think you know what hate is now?

From,
William

Extensions

- Drawing Hate: Inform students that a new dictionary will be strictly visual, so all definitions must be represented without words. Invite students to create an image or design to represent what the word *hate* means.
- Synonyms for *Hate*: There are many words to consider when we feel hate. By exploring this list of synonyms, students might better consider the degree of

The word *abhor* is from the Latin word *abhorere*, "to shrink back in horror." It can be considered the strongest way in English to express hatred.

hate that someone might feel for something or someone. Consider: Which words are students most familiar with? Not familiar with? Which words express an especially strong feeling of hate?

animosity	contempt	dislike	distaste	hostility	rancor
antagonism	disfavor	displeasure	enmity	loathing	repulsion
aversion	disgust	dissatisfaction	hatred	malice	

Lesson: The ABCs of Hate

To understand the many facets of hate, it is important that students gain key vocabulary to discuss, understand, and clarify terms connected to hate. Students can draw upon their practice with language and word power when reading, writing, and talking about stopping the hate.

These options have students explore the list presented in The ABCs of Hate on page 22.

The list of words on page 22 can be presented to students to activate prior knowledge and experience, and to have them carefully consider their assumptions. Reviewing this list independently and meeting with others to discuss the meaning of key vocabulary can prompt students to search for definitions of these words and/or to examine the glossary that appears on page 128.

Independent Reading and Inquiry

Students can work independently to review the list of words on The ABCs of Hate, page 22.
1. Have students review the list and put a dot beside (or circle) ten items they are familiar with.
2. Have students put a question mark beside 3–5 items they would like explanations for.
3. Students can use the internet or the dictionary to find definitions of vocabulary connected to hate.
4. Students can meet with a partner or in small groups to discuss their answers.

Meeting in Pairs or Small Groups

Students work with one or two classmates to review the list of words on page 22.
1. Have students share their assumptions or explanations for vocabulary they are familiar with.
2. Have students find definitions for any items that they are unfamiliar with.
3. Students can create a glossary of at least 12 items from this list. Remind students that a glossary is an alphabetical list of words with brief explanations, found in or relating to a specific subject or text.

Extensions

- Encourage students to add to the list words that might be important to understand when reading and writing about, or discussing, hate.
- The class can make an illustrated alphabet book entitled The ABCs of Hate. Each student can choose one word from the list and create an illustration that would help to visually explain the meaning of that word.
- Make copies of the glossary on page 128 available to students for reference as they continue their work on hate and discrimination.

Lesson: Is Hate the Opposite of Love?

> "The opposite of love is not hate, it's indifference."
> — Elie Wiesel

Most of us have colors we like to wear, games we like to play, authors we like to read, foods we like to eat, places we like to visit, etc. Sometimes these things are so special to us that we might say that we *love* them, especially when we think about family, friends, and, yes, pets.

Someone may say that they love to watch horror movies, while someone else hates them. Someone may love to eat broccoli, others wouldn't put it in on their plate. Some may love going to gym class, others might dread it. Our preferences and tastes differ from those around us, and these differences are part of who we are. We needn't judge a person because they don't like the same things we do. However, when those differences are matters of race, religion, sexuality, or worldviews, and we don't respect or tolerate those differences, that can lead to hate incidents. And to be compassionate, caring citizens, we need to stop the hate.

1. Have students consider things that they are passionate about and favor (like) and things that upset them (hate), and complete these sentence stems:

   I like…
   I really like…
   I love…
   I hate…

2. Students can share their responses with others in small groups and discuss:
   • Which items were similar?
   • Which items were surprises? Is hate the opposite of love?
   • What does the quotation by author and Holocaust survivor Elie Wiesel at the top of this page mean to you?

I love…

Nachos with lots of melted cheese	My Mom – she's the BEST!
Reading comics	Eating Ramen
Drawing monsters	The color Aqua
Making cupcakes	Pokemon
Papaya	Figure skating
School (on Fridays)	Camping
My cat, Misty	My grandma's voice
My puppy, Rocket	Laughing
Reading quietly in my room	Projects
K-Pop and BTS	Snowboarding
Mint chocolate chip ice cream	Blabbing on the phone
All the books by Rick Riordan	The smell of apple pie baking
Auggie Pullman (Wonder)	The Dollar Store
Freshly steamed shrimp dumplings	Word puzzles
Soccer	Winning Monopoly
Sleep, because it doesn't need work and no one can bother you	Getting an A+
	My girlfriend

I hate...
Covid-19
When people hate other
  people
Getting bullied by half the kids
  in my class
Myself
My brother's attitude
War
My body
Criticism
Spiders and bugs
Overpopulation and vegetables
Homophobic people
When my marker leaks through
  my paper
Homework
Getting injured

Calories
Rude people
Having to wear a mask
Stereotyping
Sweating on a hot hot day
Carrots (they take too long to
  chew)
Okra
Tests
Climate change
When people touch me without
  permission
The media and its false bias views
  of certain countries
Sunday evenings
Offensive jokes
Hate

Extension

After students have prepared lists of things they like and things they hate, they can transform their writing into a list poem:

1. List 10-15 items in an order you choose: e.g., alphabetically; by syllable counts; from least-favorite to strongest item.
2. Some alternatives for writing list poems:
   - Two poems presented alongside each other.
   - Alternate lines *I love…* and *I hate…* to complete a list poem; for example:

   I love the smell of fresh-baked bread;
   I hate the smell of a gym bag.

There are more than 100 songs with the word *hate* in the title: "Hate That I Love You" (Rihanna); "I Hate Myself for Losing You" (Kelly Clarkson); "I Hate Boys" (Christian Aguilera); etc.

Lesson: Opening Up About Hate: An Assumption Guide

The strategy of using an assumption guide is designed both to activate a student's background knowledge surrounding an issue and to stimulate interest and build curiosity about a topic. A list of statements about a topic is presented for students to consider and then discuss with others. The statements are intended to arouse opinions, beliefs, and attitudes about the topic.

Based on their experiences and assumptions, students might accept some statements as true. When they are asked to identify their reactions by circling their reactions (Agree, Disagree, Unsure), students are prompted to consider their own beliefs and feelings.

In this instance, the use of an assumption guide will allow students to reflect on and articulate beliefs about hate. Thinking About Hate: An Assumption Guide on page 23 can be reproduced and given to students. To begin, students independently read and respond to each of the statements; by doing so, they are confirming or challenging their opinions and beliefs. A follow-up discussion in pairs or small groups encourages students to share their views, ideas, and perhaps life stories. After listening to different opinions, some students might refine their understandings. As the discussion unfolds, students can respond to the opinions of others, raise questions, and share evidence that serves to validate their views.

Lesson: Why Do People Hate?

There is no easy answer to the questions *Why do people hate?* and *Why do some people hate other people?*

If someone is generally a positive person and willing to forgive others, the concept of hating others (whether we know them or not) might not be part of who they are. But sometimes fiery emotions fuel hatred and we may think things that are judgmental and hurtful to others. Something might have happened in someone's life that prompts them to think—and say—negative things about others. Sometimes cruel actions are taken against others. Someone might have low self-esteem or be insecure, and take out their insecurities on others, especially members of a minority. Sometimes prejudice comes from the beliefs we have been taught or from what society presents. Considering a list of reasons why some people might hate other people can help students to think about the *why*'s of hate.

1. Instruct students to work independently to answer this question in writing: *Why do some people hate others?*
2. Students meet with one or two classmates to compare reasons.
3. As a group, students compile a list of ten reasons why they think some people hate others. Once completed, have students put an asterisk (*) beside the three top reasons in answer to the question.

This list demonstrates how students from Grades 5–8 responded to the question: *Why do people hate?*

"If someone is not kind to you because you are different than them."
"When someone makes fun of them."
"When someone gives them a headache."
"Because something happened to them in their past."
"They like hating other people. It gives them power."
"They think everything someone says is questionable."
"Because they've been hated by someone else."
"Ignorant people can hate someone for their beliefs, race, sexuality, opinions."
"Info in the media about groups of people."
"They don't understand what it means to be tolerant."
"They have anger that they want to get rid of."
"They were taught that way by their families."
"They think they are superior to others race, religion, gender, size, height, etc."
"They are afraid."
"Society."
"A traumatic experience happened to them."
"I think it's because some people think that they have more power than others."
"They have a stereotypical mindset: 'All _____ people are _____ because_____.'"

In the book *Wonder* by R.J. Palacio, August Pullman's teacher Mr. Browne presents the class with words of wisdom to enlighten and comfort. The book *365 Days of Wonder* is a collection of Mr. Browne's precepts, a quote for every day of the year about courage, love, friendship, and kindness.

Consider Reasons for Hate

The Reasons for Hate handout on page 24 invites students to think about reasons for hateful behavior. Students respond to this list by prioritizing reasons they think best answer the question *Why do some people hate others?* Students can meet in groups of four or five to compare answers and provide reasons for their choices.

Lesson: Responding to Quotations

Inspirational or profound quotations can be taken as precepts to navigate and celebrate our society. They remind us that each of us has the potential to change the world, every day of the year. If we present students with inspirational quotations, we encourage them to share their personal connections to the words of others and consider what personal philosophy frames their outlook on life. Interpreting and responding to quotations provides students with opportunities to

- infer meaning behind the inspirational quotations and share their understandings with others
- consider precepts that best represent their outlook on life
- respond in a variety of modes, including writing, visual arts, drama, and media

1. Provide students with the list of quotations by philosophers, celebrities, and significant world figures on page 25.
2. Quickwrite: After independently reading the list, students choose one of the quotations and write a short response by considering the following:
   - What does this quotation mean to you?
   - Why did you choose this particular quotation?
   - What life experiences/connections does this quotation lead you to think about?
   - How is this statement inspirational for thinking about confronting hate?
3. Students meet in groups of five or six to share their chosen quotations and their responses. Groups prioritize the items, listing the most significant to the least significant in terms of the message about hate. Survey the class to determine which of the precepts was the most popular. Which quotations were not selected?

Extensions

- Gallery Walk: Display a number of quotations on walls around the classroom. Instruct students to visit each of the pieces for a moment or two to spark first impressions. If quotations are displayed on chart paper, students can record their responses and/or questions. Alternatively, sticky notes can be used for students to record and display their impressions. Following the gallery walk, the whole class can share their opinions in reaction to various quotations.
- Quotations Aloud: Students in pairs are assigned a quotation to work with. Invite students to find a way to bring this quotation to life using one or more of the following drama techniques: exploring choral dramatization, creating a still image, or using movement. Once students have rehearsed their work, they can dramatically present their quotation to others. The presentation can then be assembled into a class collective to be shared with an audience.
- Creating Posters: Students choose a quotation and create a poster or banner to display in the classroom or elsewhere in the school.
- Researching Additional Quotations: A number of quotations can be found on the internet for students to investigate and share with others.

The ABCs of Hate

These terms are related to the topic of hate. Which words and names are you familiar with? What language might you want to learn more about?

A	Activism	Agency	Assimilate
B	Bias	Bigot	
C	Cisgender	Colonize	
D	Democracy	Discrimination	Deficit Thinking
E	Equality	Equity	Ethnicity
F	Freedom		
G	Gender Identity	Genocide	
H	Harassment	Healing	Homophobia
I	Inclusion	Intersectionality	
J	Joy	Justice	
K	Kindness		
L	LGBTQ2S+		
M	Marginalized	Microaggression	
N	Nazism		
O	Oppression		
P	Prejudice	Privilege	
Q	Queer		
R	Race	Racism	Racist
S	Slur	Stereotype	Swastika
T	Transphobia		
U	Upstander		
V	Vandalism	Victim	
W	White Supremacy	Woke	
X	Xenophobia		
Y	Youth Activism		
Z	Zealot		

Thinking About Hate: An Assumption Guide

Part A: Read each statement and reflect upon it. Circle whether you agree with (A), disagree with (D), or feel unsure about (U) each statement.

1.	Hate is something that people are taught.	A	D	U
2.	Love is the opposite of hate.	A	D	U
3.	I used the word *hate* at least once this past week.	A	D	U
4.	It's always wrong to hate.	A	D	U
5.	Cyberbullying is a hate crime.	A	D	U
6.	Discrimination is a hate crime.	A	D	U
7.	Someone who hates others mostly thinks badly about themselves.	A	D	U
8.	You can teach someone not to hate others.	A	D	U
9.	I have at least one personal story about hate that I could share.	A	D	U
10.	Some social media sites promote hate.	A	D	U
11.	Education can conquer hate.	A	D	U
12.	"Sticks and stones can break my bones, but names will never hurt me."	A	D	U

Part B: Complete the following stems:

If hate were an animal, what animal would it be? Why?

When I hear the word *hate*, I think about…

If someone asked me to explain the word *hate*, I would say….

Pembroke Publishers ©2023 *Stop the Hate for Goodness Sake* by Andrew Campbell and Larry Swartz ISBN 958-1-55138-358-3

Reasons for Hate

1. Working alone, read the following list. Choose the three or four reasons you think are the most accurate. Put an asterisk (*) beside each item you choose.
2. Group Discussion: Work in groups of four to six to compare and assess your answers.
   - Which reason was the most common?
   - Which of the 10 items haven't been identified with an asterisk? Why do you think that is?
   - Can you think of additional reasons that are not on this list?

People hate because…

_____ 1. They are afraid of things that they don't know.

_____ 2. They are influenced by friends' opinions, sometimes going along with cruel things because they want to be accepted by others.

_____ 3. They absorb negative attitudes from family members.

_____ 4. They enjoy having power over others.

_____ 5. They are jealous or envious of others.

_____ 7. They hold on to what they think is "normal."

_____ 8. They are unwilling to tolerate those who are different from themselves.

_____ 9. They have had a bad experience(s) in their life that gave them opinions about others.

_____ 10. They are insecure and don't like themselves.

3. Answer the following:

How might the ideas on the list be applicable to people who are racist? Homophobic?

What might you say to someone who is being hateful to others?

Pembroke Publishers ©2023 *Stop the Hate for Goodness Sake* by Andrew Campbell and Larry Swartz ISBN 958-1-55138-358-3

Quotations About Hate

Hate has caused a lot of the problems of this world, but it has not solved one yet.
— Maya Angelou

I have decided to stick to love. Hate is too great a burden to bear.
— Martin Luther King Jr.

Once you witness an injustice, you are no longer an observer, but a participant.
— June Callwood

The opposite of love is not hate, it's indifference.
— Elie Weisel

Animals don't hate and we're supposed to be better than them.
— Elvis Presley

It's always wrong to hate, but it's never wrong to love.
— Lady Gaga

In spite of everything, I still believe that people are really good at heart.
— Anne Frank

Honestly, I don't have time to hate people who hate me, cause I'm too busy loving people who love me.
— Anonymous

No one is born hating another person because of the color of his skin, or his background, or his religion. People must learn to hate, and if they can learn hate, they can be taught to love, for love comes more naturally to the human heart than its opposite.
— Nelson Mandela

Don't hate what you don't understand.
— John Lennon

You cannot hate other people without hating yourself.
— Oprah Winfrey

Haters will say what they want but their hate will never stop you from chasing your dream.
— Justin Bieber

There is so much negativity in the world and what you only need to hear is all the love.
— Miley Cyrus

We have a choice in life—we can choose how we are going to behave. We can determine whether we reflect the good around us or lose ourselves in the darkness.
— Wab Kinew

Hate the sin, love the sinner.
— Mahatma Gandhi

Love is wise, hatred is foolish.
— Bertrand Russell

Smile more than you cry, give more than you take, and love more than you hate.
— Drake

It's time to "terminate" hatred.
— Arnold Schwarzenegger

Pembroke Publishers ©2023 *Stop the Hate for Goodness Sake* by Andrew Campbell and Larry Swartz ISBN 958-1-55138-358-3

2

Recognizing Hate

Examples of hate occur worldwide, and how hate is experienced can differ based upon where in the world we might look. Examples of racial hate or "cleansing" is common in several countries (Syria, Yemen, Iraq, China); there is systemic discrimination based on religious movements, such as Falun Gong or Tibetan Buddhists in China; systemic discrimination towards different races and sexual orientations is even more common around the globe than we sometimes experience in North America. The hate that we are most likely to encounter generally falls into one or more of the following categories: hate based on race, hate based on religion, hate based on sexual orientation or gender, and hate based on ability level. Hate occurs for many reasons, but we generally hate what we don't know and what we are taught to hate. This can take the form of outright hate crimes, discrimination, unfair treatment due to prejudice, or use of racial slurs, among other examples.

Hate Crimes

The fact that hate is on the increase is of deep concern for all. As we reflect on the hate-based violence of the past and see the hate that exists in the present, we have reason to fear that this is an indication of the future. In Canada, a country known for its diversity and acceptance, hate crimes increased by 72% overall from 2019 to 2021, a change expedited by the COVID-19 pandemic (Jain, 2022). In 2020, there was an 83% increase in race- or ethnicity-based hate crimes and a 36% increase in hate crimes overall. The next year saw a 67% increase in religion-motivated crimes, a 64% increase in hate crimes rooted in sexual orientation, and a 236% increase in hate crimes with unknown motivation (Moreau, 2022). Hate crimes in Canada targeting 2SLGBTQIA+ folks were up by 25%, a trend which has continued annually for several years (Campbell, 2022).

The FBI Hate Crime Statistics is an annual compilation of bias-motivated incidents in the United States. For the purpose of the report, a hate crime is defined as a criminal offence which is motivated, in whole or in part, by the offender's bias(es) against a person based on race, ethnicity, ancestry, religion, sexual orientation, disability, gender, and gender identity. In 2021, the Federal Bureau of Investigation (FBI) released Hate Crime Statistics 2020, an annual compilation of bias-motivated incidents in the United States, with a total of 8,263 hate crime incidents against 11,126 victims in 2020.

In the FBI statistics, 62% of victims were targeted because of the offenders' bias towards race/ethnicity/ancestry, which continues to be the largest bias motivation category: 5,227 race/ethnicity/ancestry-based incidents showed a 32% increase from 2019. Anti-Black or African American hate crimes continue to be the largest bias incident victim category, with 2,871 incidents, a 49% increase since 2019. Additionally, there were 279 anti-Asian incidents reported, a 77% increase since 2019. The other largest categories of hate crimes include anti-Hispanic or Latino incidents, with 517, and anti-White incidents, with 869 in total.

Incidents related to religion: 1,244 total incidents reported, including
- 683 anti-Jewish incidents
- 110 anti-Muslim incidents
- 15 anti-Buddhist incidents
- 89 anti-Sikh incidents

Incidents related to disability: 130 total incidents reported.
- Anti-mental disability incidents decreased by 29% since 2019
- Anti-physical disability incidents increased by 8%

Incidents related to gender and gender identity increased, with increases in gender-related incidents by 9% and gender identity-related incidents by 34%.
- 50 anti-female incidents, a decrease of 4%
- 25 anti-male incidents, an increase of 47%
- 213 anti-transgender incidents, an increase of 41%
- 53 anti-gender non-conforming incidents, an increase of 13%

A Look at Racism

"Systemic racism occurs when an institution or set of institutions working together creates or maintains racial inequity…It is often caused by hidden institutional biases in policies, practices and processes that privilege or disadvantage people based on race. It can be the result of doing things the way they've always been done, without considering how they impact particular groups differently." (Government of Ontario, 2017)

 In writing this book, my mind was called back the many times I faced marginalization due to the color of my skin as a Black man. Throughout my life, I can recall incidents where I was excluded, treated as less than, and called derogatory names due to my race. These lived examples are all evidence of racism. To come to a definition of racism, I think back to my own personal experiences and the many others shared with me by racialized school leaders, teachers, students, and community. — Andrew Campbell

There are many definitions of racism you can find in books, on the internet in equity statements, and in inclusion frameworks of school boards and organizations. However, these statements alone cannot capture the experience of racism. Racism is the intentional devaluing, exclusion, and hate shown to someone based upon race. This hatred is targeted toward those who are Black, Indigenous, and people of color. Systemic racism is the experience of this discrimination being embedded into society so that those who are classified as racialized are functionally classified as "other" or "less than," forcing them to navigate prejudice and barriers to simply exist in society.

As a country that prides itself on multiculturalism, it can be challenging to acknowledge the rampant systemic racism that persists in Canada. It is our responsibility as educators to face the truth and ensure that we do not deny the existence of racism in our schools and society.

- What evidence of hate in your community are you familiar with?
- What are some examples of hate you know about from outside your country?

- In 2021, a white educator in the Toronto District School Board wore blackface to school as a Halloween costume. The teacher was eventually asked to wash their face and a report was filed under the school board's Reporting and Responding to Racism and Hate Incidents procedure. A letter was sent home to families in which the principal acknowledged the racist and dehumanizing nature of this action and stated that disciplinary action would be taken against the teacher. (Rodrigues, 2021)
- In the Durham Catholic School Board, a new anti-racism policy was brought forward in Spring 2022. Board trustees and other stakeholders pushed back against the use of language and definitions of terms such as *white supremacy* and *colonialism*. While the document ultimately included requirements for easy reporting of racism and greater curriculum resource diversity, the pushback was significant enough for important definitions and statements on recognizing power dynamics to be excluded from the final version. (Follert, 2022)
- In 2019, a racialized Quebec hockey player left a game partway through the second period after he and his family were the repeated targets of racist comments and actions. A member of a semi-professional hockey league, this player and his family had their hair touched during the game, were called racist slurs, and were told to "go back home." Security attempted to separate the perpetrators from the family and the team owner did his best to identify the racist fans to ban them from future arena games. Several hockey players and fans were stunned to realize that this type of racist incident could occur so close to Montreal. (CBC, 2019)

These incidents, while shocking, are only a few outright examples of the systemic racism that occurs in our country and education systems daily. We must raise our awareness of racism to ensure that racist systems are actively being dismantled in our schools and to understand how to address racism when it occurs.

Consider these actions as crucial components of becoming more anti-racist:

"The journey from racism to anti-racism has to happen on many levels (individual, institutional, community, organization etc.). To be anti-racist, the easiest place to start is with personal action. We are called on to act even when we are uncertain, afraid, not fully informed, and uncomfortable." (Tolliver, 2020)

- Understanding yourself and others, and being aware of what makes you different
- Celebrating diversity
- Learning from and about each other
- Being deliberate about inclusion
- Examining your privilege and power as a person, and especially as a leader
- Unlearning assumptions, prejudice, and biases
- Avoiding bystander behavior in favor of genuine action
- Advocating for marginalized students and colleagues
- Being an anti-racist leader in your school
- Engaging in courageous conversations

How to talk to Kids about Race and Racism: Parent toolkit, Cultures of Dignity https://culturesofdignity. com/blog/guest-blogs/how-to-talk-tokids-about-race-and-racism/

As educators, this personal action is our responsibility. What actions will you take today? Conversations about racism can be tricky and the context will vary depending on who is talking and what their personal experiences with race and racism are. How To Talk to Kids about Race and Racism: Parent Toolkit, an online resource, provides expert advice for parents (and teachers). A few key points:

- *Set the example*: We need to feel comfortable discussing race and racism among ourselves.
- *Help young people navigate their curiosity*: Encourage students to ask questions about otherness as they meet it in life and in literature.
- *Make it relatable*: Sharing stories (personal, fictional, and from the media) might help students see that it can be hard for people who want society to be fair.
- *Be open about addressing mistakes*: Encourage honest communication about a put-down, rather than just calling someone a racist. Saying "Tell me more" invites opportunities to point of view.
- *Be an advocate:* Don't merely say people are equal, but act in ways that reflect that thinking.

Pause and Reflect

1. What would you do if you saw a racist or hateful act from a student?
2. How does recognizing the realities of racism in Canada make you feel? How can you actively make space to sit with feelings of discomfort to understand the realities of racism?
3. Are there assumptions, stereotypes, and biases you hold that might influence your practice as an educator? How will you take steps to unlearn them?

Anti-Black Racism

"If you live in this system of white supremacy, you are either fighting the system of you are complicit. There is no neutrality to be had towards systems of injustice, it is not something you can just opt out of." (Oluo, 2018, p. 211)

What Is Anti-Black Racism?

Anti-Black racism is prejudice, attitudes, beliefs, stereotyping and discrimination that is directed at people of African descent and is rooted in their unique history and experience of enslavement and its legacy. Anti-Black racism is deeply entrenched in Canadian institutions, policies and practices, to the extent that anti-Black racism is either functionally normalized or rendered invisible to the larger White society. Anti-Black racism is manifest in the current social, economic, and political marginalization of African Canadians, which includes unequal opportunities, lower socio-economic status, higher unemployment, significant poverty rates and overrepresentation in the criminal justice system. (Government of Ontario, 2022)

How Does Racism/Anti-Black Racism Affect Our Community?

by Andrew Campbell

Let's consider the impact that racism and anti-Black racism have on communities. The sample is based on actual responses of workshop participants. In small groups, have students create their own *jamboard* based on this example and the ideas you brainstorm.

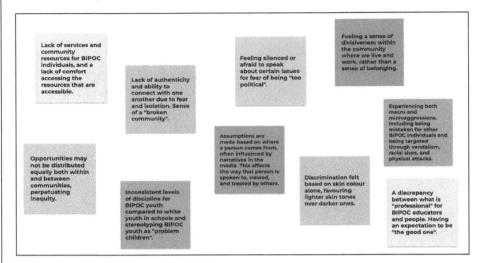

What Can We Do Better?: The Importance of Self-Reflection

One of the most important steps towards becoming anti-racist is developing a strong practice of self-reflection. We all have a responsibility to fight hate and racism whenever we see it, and we can start with ourselves. When we begin our journey towards anti-racism, we may begin in a *zone of fear*. In this stage, we deny that racism is a problem in an attempt to be comfortable, and remain ignorant towards issues of racism. To move out of this stage, we must enter the *learning zone* where we listen to those with different life experiences than our own, recognize the existence of racism, seek out questions and discussions that could bring about uncomfortable feelings, and educate ourselves by listening to BIPOC educators and individuals to understand their lived experiences and the real impacts of racism on their lives. The final stage of progression towards becoming anti-racist is the *growth zone*, in which we sit with our discomfort, actively challenge racism when it occurs, advocate for anti-racist practices and policies, and yield power roles to marginalized individuals whose voices deserve to be heard (Anti Racist Cumbria, 2021).

Consider your current status on the anti-racism trajectory. How can you advocate for anti-racism in everyday life at work and at home? What can we do better?

I See You: The Importance of Building Relationships

Many of our everyday actions lack relationships. We need to be aware of each other and see one another to create lasting change. This includes an awareness of the patterns of discrimination, inequality, and injustice that occur in schools and society. We must recognize how these patterns might show up covertly in one's community. In doing so, we must be aware of our own roles in ensuring respect for difference and fostering inclusion. A common claim for people at the beginning of their equity journey is the mentality that they do not see color. It is in fact our responsibility to see color, so that we can understand the ways that racism influences our relationships, societies, and systems. Without seeing color:

- the complexities of racial issues and the beauty of individuality can be ignored
- the struggles of BIPOC individuals can be minimized or erased
- our own prejudices cannot be recognized, and thus cannot be dismantled

(Coke, 2020)

Personal Stories about Anti-Black Hate

Dr. Marie Green is an instructor at the Ontario Institute for Studies in Education, University of Toronto, where she teaches courses in Anti-Discriminatory Education and Religious Education.

The first time I was called "the N-word" I was in Grade 9. I was still considered a new-comer to Canada, having just arrived the previous year. The expression came from a blond and blue-eyed man who was doing work on the outside of the building across the street from the housing project where my family had settled. His precise words were, "N-----, go back to where you came from." To my 14-year-old mind, his words were puzzling. "I didn't do anything to this person, I don't even know them," I thought. "Why would they want to be mean to me?" I had migrated from Jamaica with my family, and it was not my choice to leave. Other than the constant threat of home invasion due to the abject poverty that surrounded our little enclave, happy memories abounded, and I missed my grandmother dearly. The white man's verbal assault felt physical. It made me feel frightened and immediately worried that many white Canadians felt the way he did. My happy vision of a perfect and welcoming Canada was shattered in that moment. Just as I was about to lose faith in humanity, there came Ross Ornstein, my ballet teacher in secondary school. Mrs. Ornstein did more than teach me; she restored my faith in humanity. It was dance that kept my spirit afloat.

I never told anyone about the incident involving "the N-word." I didn't want to worry my already very burdened mother. Telling my siblings, who were themselves trying to adjust to our new life in Canada, would mean telling my mother. I kept it to myself, but it was not lost on me when I recalled my grandmother's words about the Lord working in mysterious ways. It mattered not to me how many rappers used the term, there was no way to normalize it into being less horrific. Even when the hateful term had been uttered against me. But there I am, still alive and dancing.

— Marie Green

My Black

They benefit from our strength, stepping on our backs to reach new heights
Infused by greed, they move like swarms of locutors across lands
Draining the earth of life, drunk with power and privilege
They plot and plan for control, fear as a weapon and shield
Determined to break our spirits by burying our stories
Attempting to keep us silent, ignoring cries for justice
They seek perfection, using false standards and measures
Claiming that my Blackness is ugly, dirty or invisible
Yet the memories live in our vein, past down from generation to generation
Beauty inherited, bestowed and nurtured by the creator
Mixed with fire, wind and water

Descended from kings and queens, and born to wear a crown
I stand before you, reborn and renew with a purpose
As proof that your sacrifice has not been lost or forgotten
Strength to stand, fight and protect
To be a leader and an agent for change
I am the link between the old and the young
The connection between the past and present
Called to be the light for our children and their children
To represent love, the only kind that matters
For the truth has been unveiled, clear as day
We will never fit their standard for our might is too great
Blackness will always be a threat, to the weak hearts and minds
Because Black is beyond perfection, because Black is greatness
Together will we rise, and transform the world
In unity we will succeed to see the future shine
Because my Black is beautiful, and Your Black is Brilliant,
Because their Black is special, and our Black is Excellence!
— by Anthonia Ikeme

Bookshelf: Picture Books Featuring the Black Identity

Africville by Shauntay Grant; illus. Eva Campbell

All Because You Matter by Tami Charles; illus. Bryan Collier (also *We Are Here*)

An American Story by Kwame Alexander; illus. Dare Coulter

A Door Made for Me by Tyler Merritt; illus. Lonnie Ollivierre

The Other Side by Jacqueline Woodson; illus. E.B. Lewis

Viola Desmond Won't Be Budged by Jody Nyasha Warner; illus. Richard Rudnicki

When We Say Black Lives Matter by Maxine Beneba Clarke

Anti-Asian Racism

What Is Anti-Asian Racism?

Anti-Asian racism refers to historical and ongoing discrimination, negative stereotyping, and injustice experienced by peoples of Asian heritage, based on others' assumptions about their ethnicity and nationality. Peoples of Asian heritage are subjected to specific overt and subtle racist tropes and stereotypes at individual and systemic levels, which lead to their ongoing social, economic, and political marginalization, disadvantage, and unequal treatment.

The word *Asian* encompasses a wide range of identities and is an umbrella term for all peoples living in the continent of Asia, encompassing East Asian people, South Asian people, and Pacific Islanders. While all may experience being "otherized," specific experiences of anti-Asian racism vary. Some are constantly being perceived to be a threat, some face gendered exotification and violence, some are more likely to be subjected to online hate and racist portrayals in the media, while others face forms of religious-based discrimination.

COVID-19, which originated in Wuhan, China, reignited anti-Asian racism. Saying that Chinese people were responsible for COVID-19 is anti-Asian hate, resulting in intolerance and some senseless crimes.

Dr. Mary Reid is an Associate Professor at the Ontario Institute for Studies in Education (OISE), University of Toronto. Mary is a first-generation settler on Turtle Island of Hakka Chinese descent. As an executive member of the Asian Canadian Educators Network (ACENet) she co-leads the research committee that focuses on examining Asian educators' and students' experiences in schools.

Have You Ever Regretted Not Speaking Up?

by Mary Reid

"Silence becomes cowardice when occasion demands speaking out the whole truth and acting accordingly."
– Mahatma Gandhi

In 2008, I landed my dream job, teaching prospective teachers at the Ontario Institute for Studies in Education (OISE). I was excited and eager to make an impact on teacher practice. Earlier that year, a Toronto councillor made headline news. He stated the following at a councillors meeting: "Those Oriental people work like dogs… they sleep beside their machines… the Oriental people, they're slowly taking over… they're hard, hard workers." While busily preparing for class, I overheard a group of teacher candidates talk about the councillor's remarks. The discussion began with disbelief that the councillor uttered the word "Oriental" and went on to explore its negative connotation—the term exoticized Asian people as forever foreigners. The discussion turned when one candidate suggested that the media overreacted, and the statement was actually a compliment to Asians because they were defined as hard-working. The group of classmates all agreed and brushed it off as sensationalized politics. When I heard this, I froze, feeling the scars that had developed over time from the discrimination and hate I encountered as an Asian female. I just didn't know how to respond. I felt compelled to go over to the group and facilitate a mini-lesson on the *model minority* myth. My heart was racing, my hands were shaking, and I didn't know how to make it a teachable moment. Class was about to begin in less than a minute, and I felt the pressure to re-direct my energies to teaching my math lesson. If only I could turn back time, if only I had the courage to speak up, if only I was equipped with anti-racism strategies. I would have walked over and joined their dialogue with honesty, kindness, and compassion.

If I were to go back in time, I would have asked the group if they were aware of the term *model minority*. In the 1960s, the term was coined by a white sociologist with the aim of intentionally inserting a wedge between marginalized groups. The misconception is grounded in the belief that if Asians can overcome barriers and succeed, then all other racialized groups should be able to do the same. Obviously, this myth doesn't take into consideration how oppression affects different groups in unique ways. In addition, prior to the 1960s, the prevalent narrative was the "Yellow Peril," in which Asians were described as savages and seen as a threat to North American society.

All too often, Asian students, educators, and community members feel invisible in educational institutions, largely due to the model minority myth. The fallacy paints all Asians as monolithic: a whole race that achieves universal academic and career success due to their innate intelligence and hard-working nature. This misconception poses harm because it renders anti-Asian racism as non-existent, which ultimately leads to the erasure of the real struggles experienced by Asian people.

Fast forward to today: I continue to purposely develop skills and strategies as an anti-racist educator. I often think about that pivotal moment of regret during my first year of teaching at OISE. Although I didn't act that day, the memory provides me with a reminder of the action I must take when confronted with microaggressions, invalidations, and microassaults. In solidarity, we can amplify our voices and shed light on the harmful effects of stereotypes. Today, I am confident to speak up when I witness behaviors that perpetuate acts of hate and discrimination. As educators, we must use our power and privilege to collectively resolve issues of inequity and embody the heartfelt work of inclusion. For it is not only the outwardly racist acts that we must fear; we must also acknowledge that our inaction and silence perpetuate injustice.

Personal Story about Anti-Asian Hate

 I am Chinese. Last year during COVID I went outside without a mask. I was just going for a walk. Then I heard two teenagers mocking the Chinese language, using funny accents. I tried to ignore them but they approached me and shouted, "Put on your mask, you Chinese virus!" After that I became paranoid if anything like that would happen again.
— Natalie F., Grade 8

Bookshelf: Picture Books Featuring Asian Identity

Eyes That Kiss in the Corners by Joanna Ho; illus. Dung Ho (Sequel: *Eyes That Speak to the Stars*)
Grandfather's Journey by Allen Say (Sequel: *Tea with Milk*)
I Am Golden by Eva Chen; illus. Sophia Diao
The Most Beautiful Thing by Kao Kalia Yang; illus. Khoa Le
My Name is Yoon by Helen Recorvits; illus. Gabi Swiatkowska
Watercress by Andrea Wang; illus. Jason Chin

Anti-Indigenous Racism

What Is Anti-Indigenous Racism?

Anti-Indigenous Racism has been part of our society for as long as "Canada" has existed. With Canada's colonist history, anti-Indigenous racism remains one of the most predominant forms of hatred, and is considered to be deeply ingrained in our daily interactions and worldviews. Addressing anti-colonist education and practices have been given stronger attention in recent years. Still, the systemic, overt, and passive racism against the Indigenous community continues to persist.

Dr. Jennifer Brant is an Assistant Professor in the department of Curriculum Teaching and Learning at The Ontario Institute for Studies in Education. Dr. Brant belongs to the Kanien'kehá:ka (Mohawk Nation) and has family ties to Six Nations of the Grand River Territory and Tyendinaga Mohawk Territory.

PERSPECTIVE

Interview with Jennifer Brant

In this interview, scholar Dr. Jennifer Brant provides insights into Indigenous education and the crucial role for teachers in advancing Truth and Reconciliation in Canada.

Q: How would you describe your approach to teaching and learning?
JB: I believe in teaching that is engaging and personally meaningful. If we want to disrupt structural and colonial violences, it is essential that we speak to the hearts and minds of learners and encourage reflexivity. To do

this, I extend Indigenous Maternal Pedagogies to foster an ethical, relational, and culturally safe teaching and learning environment to engage in critical and unsettling conversations. Indigenous Maternal Pedagogies offer a pedagogical framework that encourages anti-racist and ethical dialogue as a way to encounter difficulty, embrace vulnerability, and foster the emotional learning required to promote meaningful and transformative engagement. With this pedagogical approach in mind, I urge my students to engage in effective responses to the Truth and Reconciliation Commission of Canada's 94 Calls to Action and the 231 Calls for Justice released in the final report of the National Inquiry into Missing and Murdered Indigenous Women and Girls entitled *Reclaiming Power and Place.*

Q: What does this pedagogical approach involve?

JB: This teaching approach involves engaging students in thinking deeply about Indigenous resurgence and moving beyond superficial attempts toward reconciliation. Combatting anti-Indigenous racism and teaching the history of the residential schools of Canada means dealing with difficult, complex topics. I believe it is important to incorporate lessons on recent issues that have led to the fractured relationship between Indigenous and non-Indigenous peoples in Canada. These include, but are not limited to, ongoing racialized, sexualized, and gender-based violences against Indigenous peoples; institutional racism; cultural appropriation; and discrimination against Indigenous children. It is also important to teach from a strength-based lens that centres the sophisticated knowledges that govern Indigenous relations to our land and nonhuman kin. I find a lot of teacher candidates get stuck and feel a sense of unpreparedness to teach from a reconciliatory lens, but there is a plethora of resources out there and I intentionally curate course syllabi to introduce students to these resources. My work also positions Indigenous literatures as educational tools to move students beyond passive empathy, inspire healing and wellness, and foster socio-political action. In this way, students are equipped with the resources to develop their own teaching kits.

Q: What advice might you give to teachers to confront anti-Indigenous racism?

JB: I think it is important that teachers begin with reflexivity and understand that confronting anti-Indigenous racism is an ongoing journey. This journey involves humility and vulnerability. It is essential that we ensure all students feel that the classroom is a safe place, as they learn about the history of residential schools and its ongoing effects. Unpacking the issues and dealing with these topics can evoke strong emotions of frustration and guilt. It is important that students feel empowered to participate in class discussion.

To support a culturally safe environment, I extend the Haudenosaunee teaching of Ka'nikonhrí:io, which emphasizes the importance of bringing a good mind to all that we do, and the Anishnaabe practices of Mino-biimaadiziwinan, or living the good life through a good mind that involves a harmonious balance of the mind, body, and spirit (Anderson, 2005). For example, the idea of the good mind can be applied in the classroom by encouraging students to be respectful of one another's worldviews and ways of being, and to consider their own role in reconciliation. Change begins with education. Whether in elementary, secondary, or university

See page 136 for Dr. Brant's suggestions for teachers to begin curating their own classroom libraries.

classrooms, it is important to look within and confront preconceived notions and biases.

Q: Why, in your opinion, is this education important?

JB: For a very long time, Indigenous content was left out of education altogether or presented in harmful and stereotypical ways. These stereotypes fuel the violences that target Indigenous peoples today. As a child in school, I never saw reflections of my cultural identity, family traditions, or the vast contributions of Indigenous communities. Whenever Indigenous content was presented—which was rarely—it was done in stereotypical and harmful ways. To confront, prevent, and respond to anti-Indigenous racism, teachers need to be committed to changing this reality. Teaching Indigenous content from a strength-based lens, along with lessons about Indigenous experiences of racism and settler colonialism, is necessary if we want to dismantle anti-Indigenous racism. I truly believe change begins with education, and that Indigenous content must be introduced with an intentional pedagogy and process that identifies and dismantles anti-Indigenous racism.

Personal Story about Anti-Indigenous Hate

Whilst taking my Masters degree at a well-known University, each person in our cohort needed to present about their intended thesis. I spoke about the Sixties Scoop, of which I am a survivor, a policy that enabled child welfare authorities to take or "scoop up" Indigenous children from their families and communities and place them for adoption in non-Indigenous households. Some of the cohort firmly stated that they believed this never happened—the Canadian government would never do this; I was making it up. My advisor, sitting in the room, said nothing. Nobody defended the truth that day. Nobody objected to the denial of what was said. That experience hurt very much, as it was the first time I had spoken publicly about the Sixties Scoop. Nobody stood or objected. All that had formed my life was negated that day. Since then, although I have run into many of those people, nobody has ever apologized or spoken about it.

— John Doran, PhD.

Megweg Mik'chich'k Jin'm

Sipkne'katik District, Mi'kmaw Nation

Bookshelf: Picture Books Featuring Indigenous Identity

Fry Bread: A Native American Family Story by Kevin Noble Maillard; illus. Juana Martinez-Neal

Shi-shi-etko by Nicola Campbell; illus. Kim LaFave (Sequel: *Shin-chi's Canoe*)

Still This Love Goes On by Buffy Sainte-Marie; illus. Julie Flett

Stolen Words by Melanie Florence; illus. Gabrielle Grimard

We Are Water Protectors by Carole Lindstrom; illus. Michaela Goade (also *Berry Song* by Michaela Goade)

When We Were Alone by David A. Robertson; illus. Julie Flett (also *On The Trapline*)

When I Was Eight by Christy Jordon-Fenton and Margaret Pokiak-Fenton; illus. Gabrielle Grimard (Sequel: *Not My Girl*)

A Look at Religion-Based Hate

Religion is another common cause of hate incidents, with over a third of Canadian hate crimes in 2018 being religion-based (Swan, 2020). Religious hate crimes can be committed against a person or a place and include both personal attacks and violence towards religious institutions. The fear stemming from religious-based hate can cause people to fear identifying themselves with a religion or sharing their true beliefs. People might also feel afraid to attend their place of worship due to acts of hate, such as shootings at synagogues and mosques. These terrible acts of hate based on religion can cause people to live in fear or distress due to their beliefs, which are a fundamental part of who they are.

Antisemitism

What Is Antisemitism?

> Coined in the late nineteenth century, the term antisemitism (l'antisemitisme) was applied directly to hatred of Jews and not of all Semitic peoples. Today, antisemitism refers to latent or overt hostility or hatred directed towards individual Jews or the Jewish people—that is, anti-Jewish oppression—leading to social, economic, institutional, religious, cultural or political discrimination. Antisemitism has also been expressed through individual acts of harassment, physical violence, vandalism, the organized destruction of entire communities and genocide. (from *Addressing Hate Crimes in Ontario*, 2006)

Antisemitism is a certain perception of Jews that can be expressed as hatred towards Jews. Antisemitism frequently charges Jews with conspiring to harm humanity and it is often used to blame Jews for "why things go wrong." It is expressed in speech, writing, visual forms, and actions, and employs sinister stereotypes and negative character traits. It is also called Jew-hate; Jew-hatred, and anti-Jewish racism. (from *Unlearn It*, 2022)

Unlearn It is an online platform launched to address Jew-hatred in schools, providing information and strategies to learn about, identify, and take action to address antisemitism. The Unlearn It tools 1) for Educators and 2) for Parents can be used proactively as part of anti-racism programming or reactively when an incident occurs in the school and/or community.

Kathy Kacer is the author of a number of Holocaust Remembrance books:
The Secret of Gabi's Dresser; The Brave Princess and Me (picture book) illus. Juliana Kolesova; *Broken Strings* (with Eric Walters); *The Brushmaker's Daughter; Under the Iron Bridge; To Hope and Back: The Journey of the St Louis*

PERSPECTIVE

Combatting Antisemitism

by Kathy Kacer

It has often been said that the Holocaust did not begin with the killing of Jews in the gas chambers. It began with words—hateful words and hateful symbols like the swastika—that alienated and targeted Jews across Europe. The cases of swastikas appearing on school walls in North America is becoming an alarming trend. Stats Canada in 2019 reported that antisemitic crimes against Jewish people accounted for the highest number of religion-based hate crimes in the country. In 2020, the number increased even more. (Dorcas Marfo, *Toronto Star*, Reb. 8, 2022)

What can educators do to try to combat these incidents? First and foremost, you need to report these crimes (and yes, they are crimes) to your local police unit. The police must be informed when antisemitic acts occur. Those responsible must be held accountable. But it's not enough just to punish the offenders.

Holocaust education is still key in helping students understand how hate begins, and how words and symbols can fuel the situation. Bring a Holocaust survivor into your classroom to talk with your students. Let them hear the stories from the mouths of those who experienced the full impact of hate. Ask the survivor how he or she feels when they see a swastika painted on the wall of a building. Their emotional response will stay with you and your students forever.

Do this sooner rather than later! Holocaust survivors are passing away at an alarming rate and it will not be long before their voices are gone. Contact your local synagogue, Holocaust centre, or Jewish community centre to find a survivor who fits with the age and stage of your student group.

If you can't find a survivor who will speak to your students, consider bringing in an author—someone like me, who is the child of Holocaust survivors and has written books about this time in history for a young readership. Authors can help initiate students into this history in a gentle and encouraging way. We are waiting for the opportunity to do that.

Provide stories from the past of those who stood up for their Jewish friends and neighbors. The stories of helpers and rescuers is critically important, celebrating those brave individuals who demonstrated good citizenship and moral courage at that dangerous time in history. These courageous people can be role models for your students as they grapple with understanding the impact of hate. Challenge your students to find ways to be caring citizens in their own neighborhood or school—how they can act with compassion and have empathy and respect for everyone.

My late friend and Holocaust survivor Werner Reich once told me that when he spoke to students in schools, he left them with one task. They had to do something positive in their community and they had to write to him and tell him about that act of kindness. He received thousands of letters. Some were quite amusing—a student wrote that they walked the dog without being asked! Most were memorable, describing how they helped an elderly neighbor, or contributed time or money to a worthy cause, or intervened when a friend was being bullied. It may seem like an uphill battle to combat hate. But Werner always said that the letters he received from young people made it well worth the while.

Personal Stories about Antisemitism

 I know the victim of this hate-crime and was chilled to learn about this disturbing antisemitic incident.

See B'nai Brith media release, September 15, 2021 https://www.bnaibrith.ca/toronto-man-charged-in-brutal-antisemitic-assault/ and *Toronto News*, September 18, 2021 https://www.toronto.com/news/jewish-organization-calls-for-action-following-anti-semitic-violence-in-torontos-west-end/article_d1ef35d0-08cc-56e5-a4d3-ec196a746daa.html?

A man walked into a store and assaulted a member of the staff both physically and verbally. The elderly Jewish employee asked the man to produce identification to show he was of legal age to buy alcohol. After hurling an antisemitic comment about the clerk's name, the customer struck the worker in the back of the head with a wine bottle, continued to throw other items, and then punched the employee in the face. The Jewish clerk was knocked unconscious and required stitches. Police officers investigated the incident as a hate-motivated crime. The assailant was subsequently arrested.

— Larry Swartz

I didn't experience antisemitism growing up in Arizona, but I had a major experience with it completing high school in Northern California. Friends would always call me by my last name. So the sound of Jewishness always rang in my ear when my friends would call across the hallway, "Hey, Spielberg!" and I was very well conscious of that.
— Steven Spielberg, *New York Times*, Sunday November 13, 2022

Bookshelf: Picture Books featuring Jewish Identity
The Brave Princess and Me by Kathy Kacer; illus. Juliana Kolesova (also *The Magician of Auschwitz*)
Chick Chak Shabbat by Mara Rockliff; illus. Krysten Brooker
Here Is the World by Lesléa Newman; Illus. Susan Gal
The Prisoner and the Writer by Heather Camlot; illus. Sophie Casson (YA)
The Promise by Pnina Bat Zvi and Margie Wolfe; illus. Isabelle Cardinal
Yaffa and Fatima: Shalom, Salaam by Fawzia Gilani-Williams; illus. Chiare Fedele

Islamophobia

What Is Islamophobia?

Islamophobia is the fear of, hatred of, or prejudice against the religion of Islam or Muslims. Some experts consider Islamophobia to be a form of racism or xenophobia, while some argue that religion is not a race. Islamophobia increased as a result of the September 11 attacks, other terror attacks in Europe and the United States by Islamic extremists, and the increased presence of Muslims settling in Europe and the United States. Islamophobia connotes a societal anxiety, namely fear, about Islam and Muslims. Globally, statistics reveal that many Muslims report not feeling respected by those in the West. There are more than two billion Muslim people in the world, living in different countries, speaking different languages, and wearing different traditional clothing. Some people, due to fear, ignorance, and stereotyping, think all Muslims are the same.

Additional terms that refer to negative feelings and attitudes towards Islam and Muslims include *anti-Muslimism, intolerance against Muslims, anti-Muslim prejudice, anti-Muslim bigotry, Muslimophobia, anti-Islamism.*

The Greek Suffix phobia is used in English to form nouns with the sense of "fear of…" or "aversion to…"

@studentAsim is the author of several picture book publications centred on social justice, equity, and diversity. Titles include *My Skin: Brown*; *Khadijah Goes to School: A story about you*; and *The Tyer of Ties*.

PERSPECTIVE

Is it possible to make a difference against Islamophobia even if it's not your experience?

by @studentAsim

As a little boy, I loved good and avoided danger. Good was play and sincere people. Danger was bullying and racism.

Growing up in my community of York, life was connected to faith, culture, play, and education. I enjoyed going to the mosque; with only one in all of Toronto at the time, many would travel there and gather, as it was a central meeting point. I remember all the good people—teachers, friends, and people from the Islamic community. I admired older youths and wanted them to like me, it felt so special.

That was one of the best periods of my life. But things aren't the same anymore.

In today's world, I'm often reminded that I'm Muslim, a societal experience that isn't always positive. The racism I experienced as a little boy is more complex now; it was skin color back then. Today, it's exacerbated by religious labels and tropes that constrain how the world is perceived for some groups. For Muslims, it's a world where we now have a National Day of Remembrance of the Québec City Mosque Attack and Action against Islamophobia on January 29th each year.

In my Canada, I never thought there would come a day to remember victims of crimes targeted just for being Muslim. Seventeen children were left fatherless in that deadly mosque massacre. In London, Ontario, a man rammed his truck into Muslim Pakistani pedestrians, killing four people—three generations of the same family—while they were out for a family walk. There are countless other stories, some that have had media coverage, and a lot more that haven't or never will.

Each story is important.

I'm thinking back to me as a boy going to day camp and just being me. But to then grow up to witness this?

In the days after London, the country was once again confronted with the question the Muslim community knew far too well: "How could this happen?" In thinking about these horrors of hateful crimes, we might ask, "Is it possible to make a difference against Islamophobia, especially when it might not be directly part of your culture or faith?"

Understandably, if Islam isn't your religion, or if you don't go beyond the formalities of knowing Muslims, it's true, it's not part of your experience. However, when we speak of systems like education or government serving people, not knowing enough about minority groups like Muslims—who are stereotypically judged—can act as a barrier to understanding them and helping them reach their potential. However, what if those barriers could come down and the public *could* participate with the Muslim community to actively learn about them, and to even counter Islamophobia in a simple way?

In looking for a simple solution to help the public rapidly gain context of Muslims, and communities seen as Muslim, targeted by Islamophobia, I turned to digital technologies. I designed islamophobia.io—a global web platform that gives agency to Muslims, allies, and the general public to tell memorable stories of Muslims and Islamic culture through digital storytelling. It is a counter-narrative tool where first-hand stories from said communities bust narrow definitions of Islamic-related experiences. Stories are diverse, and provide critical nuance from within, giving the public a more realistic view of Muslims, those seen as Muslim, and allied experiences to foster (often new) understanding.

Story submissions create outreach, and can easily be read and shared independently. You are invited to write stories too! There is no need for fancy writing skills or a polished resume, reinforcing islamophobia.io's objective to provide access to anyone who wants to make a difference.

I've received incredible stories and ran two national campaigns in 2022. I'd like to share some goals and results of what I learned since I launched the platform:.

Goals
- Ease: Provide an "instant" social solution to counter Islamophobia.
- Agency: Prove that anyone—not just Muslims—can counter Islamophobia.

- Instant change: Make change through digital technologies.
- Rapid context: Harness the power of storytelling to foster understanding of Muslim communities (and those seen as Muslim).
- Counter-narrative: Provide a platform that helps Muslims and allied communities tell stories in their own words.
- Storybank: Create a central repository of stories, easily accessible for rapid context-building, research, and instant change-making.

Results
- Response: The platform has received stories from people from as young as 7 and as old as 90 years old.
- Change: People (of multiple faiths/backgrounds) largely didn't plan on making change, but did with islamophobia.io as a new pathway.
- Practicality: People implemented islamophobia.io's storytelling concept easily in their existing programs.
- International scope: Digital stories have no borders; stories were submitted from all over the world.
- Simplicity: The simple site design increased engagement and, hence, enabled change.

I invite you to try https://islamophobia.io. Tell a story. Save a life.

Personal Stories about Islamophobia

Before I came to this school, I was one out of two Muslims in my grade. The other Muslim was my best friend and we always played with two other kids from foreign countries. Every day when we arrived at school, an older kid always bullied the four of us. We wanted to stand up for ourselves but we were too scared. He made fun of me because I'm Muslim and I'm from Afghanistan. This older kid called me and my friend terrorists. I felt lots of hate for this person and wished I were bigger and braver so I could bully him. — A.B., Grade 6

I know this one girl that goes to my public school, she is a young hijabi girl (Mashallah). While she was eating, minding her own business, three guys in her class thought that it was a good idea to pull her hijab off. Her hair was shown. While she tried to cover it and run, everybody was surrounding her and laughing. At the end, the boys got in trouble, gave her her hijab back, and apologized. I wonder why they were being so mean. I wonder if girls wearing hijabs lie in fear of being taunted by others. — A.L., Grade 8

This happened during the holiest month in the Islamic calendar. Hundreds of people were packed for prayers. My father was helping out in the parking area and was approached by a man on a motorcycle who turned to my father and said, "This place will be gone. I'm going to blow this place up." This man hated us for who we were and tried to put our lives in danger. Luckily he disappeared, but people like him are out there. Nobody in any country should feel unsafe based on their religious beliefs. — B.H., Grade 8

Bookshelf: Picture Books Featuring Islam and Muslim Identity
Crescent Moon and Pointed Minarets: A Muslim book of shapes by Hena Khan; illus. Mehrodokht Amini

In My Mosque by M.O. Yuksel; illus. Hatem Aly
My Name is Bilal by Asma Mobin-Uddin; illus. Barbara Kiwak
My Skin: Brown @studentAsim; illus. Sari Richter
The Proudest Blue by Muhammad Ibtihaj, with S.K. Ali; illus. Aly Hatem (also *The Kindest Red*)
Yo Soy Muslim: A father's letter to his daughter by Mark Gonzales; illus. Mehrdokht Amini

A Look at Hate Based on Sexuality and Gender Identity

"Your happiness cannot be based on my silence."
— DR.ABC

 I grew up in Jamaica afraid of anyone discovering that I was gay. From the age of six, I knew that I was different from others, and I also recognized that I needed to keep this difference silent and secret. In my book *The Invisible Student in the Jamaican Classroom*, I outline the widespread nature of homophobia in Jamaican schools, with acts of hate ranging from slurs to outright abuse, and explore school as the most common setting for queer hate, exclusion, and discrimination to occur. Experiences of hate at school include name-calling, bullying, damaged property, physical assault, and sexual assault. This is not surprising, given how many hours a day students spend in school. — Andrew Campbell

Discrimination and violent crime motivated by hate causes queer people to live in fear of being themselves and living their truth. In North America today, this might show up as racial slurs, losing friends because of one's sexual orientation, denial of the rights of transgender people, and mass shootings at queer nightclubs. This hate happens in many countries and classrooms today, and there are still too many countries where 2SLGBTQIA+ people live in fear due to hate. Anxiety, depression, shame, disengagement, and self-harm are all potential reactions to living through hate, as abuse pushes queer populations into silence and shame. In schools, queer students might live in silence and fear of expressing who they truly are. It is disheartening to consider how challenging the learning process and engagement might be for students who are surrounded by hate in a setting that should exist to further their learning and build community.

Homophobia and Hate Based on Sexuality

What Is Homophobia?
Homophobia is the fear, hatred, or intolerance of people who are homosexual. Homophobia can stem from a fear of associating with gay and lesbian people and/or of being perceived as gay or lesbian. Homophobic behaviors can range from (and beyond) telling jokes about lesbian, gay, or queer people to physical violence against people thought to lesbian, gay, or queer. Too often, students toss out the put down, "That's so gay!" or use the terms *fag, faggot*, or *lezbo*, possibly to hurt others, or perhaps they speak without thinking. The put-downs might come from ignorance, from insecurity, or from fear.

A study by Taylor and Peter (2011) that surveyed LGBTQ students tells us that 70 percent of the students reported hearing expressions such as "That's so gay" every day at school or hearing the words "fag," "faggot," "lezbo," and "dyke" almost daily. More than one in five LGBTQ students reported being physically assaulted or harassed about their perceived sexual orientation or gender identity.

Sarah Stapleton (she/ they) is a teacher candidate at OISE/UofT.

PERSPECTIVE

Showcasing Queer Joy

by Sarah Stapleton

As a queer person who experiences fluidity of both gender and sexuality, many of my school experiences were isolating and confusing. I recall inventing male-coded names for people I had crushes on as an adolescent to safely participate in conversations with peers, listening to teachers use the phrase "boys and girls" and recognizing that I may not always belong, and hearing homophobic jokes in the hallways with nothing done about it. Although I was fortunate to have many supportive friends and teachers, it was clear to me that my full self was not welcome in all spaces.

The needs of 2SLGBTQIA+ students are essential for educators to consider when developing classrooms and school cultures that are inclusive, safe, and rooted in anti-hate philosophies. Without this consideration, queer students may experience fear, anxiety, and trauma, all of which can lead to fight–flight–freeze shutdown responses that are incompatible with true learning. Queer learners deserve a hate-free experience in the classroom, which can only be achieved through inclusive education and teacher support. Students are more than their role as learners; they are human beings learning to navigate the world. As such, they need accurate information about different genders, sexualities, and family structures to prepare them for the diversity they will encounter in their lives. Students need exposure to diverse resources and media in all classes, accurate and scientifically based sex education, and support, advocacy, and allyship from all school staff to foster and sustain safety in the classroom, hallways, schoolyard, and beyond.

Allied educators can begin this equity work by having more conversations with queer people in order to foster mutual respect, listening, and learning. Relationship-building is a foundational component of anti-hate, and it is through truly knowing others that we see diversity for the wonderful and magical force it is. Practice using different pronouns, including multiple pronouns, and learn them alongside your students' names. Consider distributing a survey with diverse pronoun options and contexts. This gives students the autonomy to use a particular pronoun in the safety of the classroom before coming out at home. Check in with the media and resources that are available in your classroom. Do textbooks feature exclusively cisgender people, heterosexual couples, and nuclear family structures? Bring in or create resources featuring nonbinary characters, lesbian couples, adopted children, and other diverse human beings. Recognize that this is not over-sexualizing curriculum, as pronouns, families, and relationships are presented in schools at every stage of education and in all classes. Use inclusive language such as "students" over gendered terms, and "family" or "guardians" rather than "Mom" and "Dad." Our worldview manifests through language, and these simple shifts create a more inclusive space.

Finally, ensure that you are showcasing queer joy in the classroom. While it is important to make space for fear when hate-based events occur, it is equally important to highlight successful queer role models and celebrate the joy queerness brings. Leading with love for all students and celebrating their uniqueness is the pathway to ending hate in our schools.

Personal Stories about Homophobia

You can't judge someone by the way they wanna dress or the way someone wants to be, because everyone is different. Sometimes homophobia can lead to tragedy. My cousin Evan got made fun of a lot by his friends and his family for being gay. In 2015 he passed away. Police officers found him at the bottom of a bridge in Portugal with his car doors open. He committed suicide. So no matter if someone is different, don't make fun of them because the worst can happen to them. RIP, Evan.
— S.L., Grade 7

This piece is an excerpt from the book *The Invisible Student in the Jamaican Classroom* by Andrew Campbell (2018).

Who is he? He gets up to get ready for school—but is fearful to go today. He knows today, like all the other days, he will have to exert so much energy to appear "normal" and be accepted by the other boys. He has to play his role and not for one minute give away what he is thinking or feeling inside. School can be a dangerous place for a boy who is so different, and he knows that too well.

Who is he? He knows he has to put on the same uniform as the other boys, but he knows deep down he is not like the other boys. He is different—not the special kind of admired different—just different. A different that is hated. The kind of different that has become a burden. The kind of different he wished he could give back. Why was he selected to be different? In a school of more than 2500 boys who wore the same uniform, attended the same classes, ate in the same cafeteria, attended the same religious assemblies and taught by the same teachers—he was selected to be different. He questions God. He questions himself since there is no one else he can ask these questions. He wants answers but is scared of the answers themselves. The questions make him sad—they make him angry. Who is responsible for making him so different?

Who is he? He is that boy who must prepare himself mentally and emotionally if he will be going to the canteen or playing on the field today. He must be ready to walk like a man, deepen his voice and be careful that he does not bend his wrist. He is that boy who must navigate the school halls to survive—he must not be in the bathroom when it is crowded. He is that boy who is fearful of bathing after gym since the male bathroom is no place for faggots, a sissy, and sure not a battyman—so once again, he brings a letter to the teacher, a forged one, asking to be excused from physical education class.

Who is he? He is that boy who is excluded from so many activities. He made that choice. It is better for him to stay away and stay out of trouble. He is obvious, he is noticed. Everything about him has become the target of ridicule. His walk, his voice, his love and passion for things that the "regular" boys do not engage in. He wished he was older, so he could understand the meaning of those words he hears being used by his teachers, the school counsellor and the principal. Words like *tolerance, acceptance, difference, otherness, inclusion* and *self-esteem*. He knows they are hypocrites, but he dares not say that. He knows his place and he keeps in his place. A school is a dangerous place for a boy like him, and he knows it.
— Andrew Campbell

Bookshelf: Picture Books Featuring Homosexual Characters

And Tango Makes Three by Justin Richardson and Peter Parnell; illus. Henry Cole

Heather Has Two Mommies by Lesléa Newman; illus. Laura Cornell

Mom and Mum Are Getting Married by Ken Setterington; illus. Alice Priestly

A Plan for Pops by Heather Smith; illus. Brooke Kerrigan

Worm Loves Worm by J.J. Austrian; illus. Mike Curato

Transphobia

What Is Transphobia?

Transphobia is irrational fear of, aversion to, or discrimination against transgender people. Transphobia, or transmisia, is when people have deeply-rooted negative beliefs and attitudes about what it means to be transgender, nonbinary, and gender nonconforming. These beliefs and attitudes affect the way individuals, the government, organizations, the media, and society generally treat people whose identities don't fit into typical gender roles.

Basically, *Transphobia* and *transmisia* are the same thing. However, the *phobia* in *transphobia* means "fear." In medical language, phobias are a type of anxiety disorder that can have a significant influence on someone's life. But attitudes, beliefs, and behaviors that hurt or erase an experience or deny the existence of trans and nonbinary people are not considered a mental-health condition. It could be unfair to people who actually have phobias to call transphobia and homophobia *phobias*. It might make it seem like it's acceptable when a person or system stigmatizes or harms trans and nonbinary people. On the other hand, the *misia* in *transmisia* means "hatred." This makes the term more helpful, because it highlights the prejudice at the root of behavior. While someone might also have some fear about trans and nonbinary people—like fear of the unknown or fear of a changing world—it isn't a phobia.

PERSPECTIVE

Allyship: Walking in Solidarity with 2SLGBTQI+ students

by Lindsay Cavanaugh

Lindsay Cavanaugh is a PhD. candidate at the Ontario Institute for Studies in Education and a certified intermediate/senior teacher. She researches femme-inist, queer, and trans educational futurities.

Allyship is defined by The Anti-Oppression Network (2021) as "an active, consistent, and arduous practice of unlearning and re-evaluating, in which a person in a position of privilege and power seeks to operate in solidarity with a marginalized group." While allyship does take work, this work is part of our responsibility to ensure that all students are safe enough to learn and grow at school. Allyship is needed throughout all dimensions of education, from classroom culture, to resources, to interactions with students and their families. It is a lifelong process that requires continual learning and growth. Most importantly, allyship is authentic and not performative. It is demonstrated through genuine care and concern for students, as well as by celebration of difference, not by attending meetings and putting a rainbow flag on the door without doing the real work. How are you inviting your students to fully participate in school, at recess, and in society as their full authentic selves? How are you investing in the creation of brave spaces so that your students know they do not need to hide parts of their identity for fear of shame, exclusion,

See page 136 for references and resources.

or bullying? Your 2SLGBTQI+ students may have witnessed hate in the world for their identities through bullying, the media, or even their families. How are you actively supporting their healing and fostering joy?

Activism Through Action

> "Allies are some of the most effective and powerful voices of the LGBT movement. Not only do allies help people in the coming-out process, they also help others understand the importance of equality, fairness, acceptance and mutual respect." (GLAAD, 2007)

As an ally, you hold significant power in not only your students' educational journeys, but their lives. These are a few of the many actions you might take to establish a culture of allyship at school:

- Actively listen to your 2SLGBTQI+ students, friends, and colleagues. Learn who they are as individuals and what they need to be successful and supported. Create the conditions to make those things happen.
- Ensure that your curriculum is reflective of the many genders, sexualities, and family structures that exist in the world, to celebrate diversity for your students and yourself.
- Prioritize learning the preferred names and pronouns of the people in your life, as well as the contexts in which they use them. Find methods of learning this information that are accessible and safe, such as written surveys or private conversations. Don't assume that anyone is straight or cisgender, and ensure that your students are not being outed to someone before they are ready.
- Call out misrepresentations, hatred, and stereotyping of 2SLGBTQI+ people and acknowledge the harm they cause. Defend these populations from discrimination and speak up when you witness it occurring.

As you continue your lifelong journey of allyship and celebration, consider the following acrostic for some additional actions you might take:

> **A**dvocacy: Advocate for your 2SLGBTQI+ friends, colleagues, family members, and students in all settings and contexts. Do not let your allyship be conditional.
> **L**eadership: Act as a leader for equity and anti-discriminatory education.
> **L**ove: Teach and act from a place of love at all times. All students deserve to receive love and care. Celebrate love in all its forms and between all genders.
> **Y**ourself: Know yourself and do your own work to evaluate and challenge the biases you hold.
> **S**olidarity: Stand up for and alongside 2SLGBTQI+ people in all circumstances.
> **H**ealing: Provide space and opportunities for healing from the harm that discrimination and exclusion can cause.
> **I**dentity: Celebrate the uniqueness of each person's identity and intersectionality.
> **P**ride: Be proud of yourself and each of your students for who they are.

Allyship is never finished. Students must always know that they are safe, cared for, and celebrated.

This personal story illustrates a scenario in which allyship is lacking. Consider the actions you might take in a similar situation, and whether these actions align with the dimensions of allyship.

Personal Story about Transphobia

My name is Eva Simone and I am a transgenderwoman. However, as a baby, the name my parents gave to me was Mark. This is because, when I was born, the doctor and my parents assumed that I was a boy because of the body I was born in, a body which usually suggests that I should be a boy. So based on the information they had of me at that time, I was assigned male sex at birth and automatically designated boy gender-identity.

As I grew up, almost everyone around me would kept telling me to "be a boy" instead of who I was naturally being. As much as they kept telling me to, I didn't know what it meant to be a boy. I became very confused and frustrated, and thought there was something wrong with me being the only me I knew myself to be. As time went by, I began to recognize the difference in social behaviors and expectations from others between someone who was born assigned male sex at birth and someone born assigned female sex at birth. I then became sad, confused, and even sometimes angry, and was afraid to be the only me I knew myself to be. As much as I tried to be the boy people wanted me to be, nothing about me changed to fit what is expected of a boy, and that feeling of something being wrong with me became even more real in my mind. I became very self-conscious, withdrawn and shy.

At night before going to sleep I would often say a prayer, asking that I would wake up being in a female-sex–assigned-at-birth body instead of my own male-sex–assigned body; so that the body I lived in would align with who I was naturally being.

At that time of my life, I did not have the language, the space, nor the courage to say who I really was. I was not even aware that I had the option to rightfully identify. It was a very frustrating and angst-centred time of my life. I often felt so alone and misunderstood.

But as I became an adult and moved from the Caribbean to Canada, I found a Community of 2SLGBTQIA-people who embraced, informed, and affirm who I really am. I finally learned the language to say how I experience and live my gender identity. Now, I identify as a transgenderwoman; which means, though I was born assigned male sex at birth, I experience and live gender as a girl/woman. An over-simplistic analogy of what that means is this: in general, most people are born with their right hand as the dominant hand they use to write or catch a ball. However, every now and then someone is born with their left hand being their dominant hand. It doesn't mean that something is wrong with them. It just means they use a different dominant hand than most people do.

As we evolve as a human family, we are learning that gender is not binary, but is more realistically a spectrum. What that means is not everyone experiences and lives gender solely based on the body they were born in. And though most people identify exclusively as man or woman, like the different shades and colors in a box of crayons are the different identities between men and women. Each person should get to identify as who they really are inside.
— Eva Simone

Bookshelf: Picture Books Featuring Gender Identity
The Boy & the Bindi by Vivek Shraya; illus. Rajini Perera
I Am Jazz by Jessica Herthel and Jazz Jennings; illus. Shelagh McNicholas
Jack (Not Jackie) by Erica Silverman; illus. Holly Hatam
Julián Is a Mermaid by Jessica Love (Sequel: *Julián at the Wedding*)
Morris Micklewhite and the Tangerine Dress by Christine Baldacchino; illus. Isabelle Malenfant
When Aidan Became a Brother by Kyle Lukoff; illus. Kaylani Juanita

A Look at Ableism

> "I was born a little different, I do my dreaming from this chair, I
> pretend it doesn't hurt me when people point and stare."
> — Allen Shamblin and Steve Seskin, *Don't Laugh At Me*

Physical ableism is hate or discrimination based on physical disability. Sanism, or mental ableism, is discrimination based on mental health conditions and cognitive disabilities.

Ableism is defined as discrimination and social prejudice in favor of able-bodied people. It is based on the belief that typical abilities are superior. At its heart, ableism is rooted in the assumption that disabled people require "fixing" and defines people by their disability. Ableism can include these attitudes towards people with disabilities:

- believing they have less value and worth
- assuming they want to be "healed" or can "overcome" a disability
- suggesting they are "inspirational" for handling everyday activities and routine tasks
- assuming they lead an unhappy, limited life

See Chapter 5: Physical and Mental Challenges in *Teaching Tough Topics* by Larry Swartz for a version of some of the material in this section.

About 6 percent of children ages 5 to 15 have disabilities, and most of them attend our schools. Our students may know someone in their classroom, in the classroom next door, or in their school and community population who is different because of their disabilities. That unique person might even be a member of their own family. According to the World Health Organization, about one in five people 15 years and over has at least one disability that limits them in their daily activities; this fact supports the idea that our students know personally someone who has a common disability, perhaps a physical disability, vision impairment, deafness, autism spectrum disorder, or cerebral palsy. Students may, thereby, have an opportunity to gain an authentic understanding of what it means to be physically or mentally different.

Disability is now understood as a human rights issue. Social justice is a way of seeing the world, interacting with people, and taking action aimed at removing barriers to equity and human rights. Social justice, freedom, and inclusion for all are priorities. So our classrooms need to be places of inclusion, based on principals of acceptance, ensuring that students with physical and mental challenges feel that they are not discriminated against and that they are a part of the school environment. Ensuring accessibility for these students is required by law. Providing a safe space where they are free from being taunted because of their differences complies with the principles of social justice, diversity, and equity learning. Like hate, inclusion of those with disabilities needs to be carefully taught.

PERSPECTIVE

Inclusion in the Classroom

by Larry Swartz

Choosing Inclusive Language
When speaking of disabilities, some words might not be considered politically correct; they are thought to be inappropriate because they exclude, marginalize, or insult people. Students need to learn to choose words that are inclusive or accepted by the people described by them. It is important to explain to our students that it is okay to use words or phrases such as *disability*, *disabled*, or *people with disabilities* when talking about disability issues. However, advise students that it is better to emphasize a person's abilities, not limitations.

To help build understanding of appropriate, inclusive language, provide students with a list of negative vocabulary and discuss why each of these terms might offend someone who has a disability.

handicapped/the handicapped	suffers from…
special	confined to a wheelchair
cripple	crazy
invalid	insane
mental	

Challenging Assumptions

Since the publication of the novel *Wonder* by R.J. Palacio in 2012, the character August "Auggie" Pullman has become an iconic fictional hero. Auggie is unique not just because of the facial deformity he was born with, but also for his courage, his determination, and his I-just-want-to-be-normal outlook on life. On the novel's first page, he shares a wish that he "could walk down the street without people seeing me and doing that look-away thing." At the end of the book, Auggie wins an award for displaying qualities that define us as human beings: Kindness, Courage, Friendship, Character.

Auggie has become the model of fictional—and real—people who learn to embrace life and demonstrate these positive human qualities. Characters like Auggie serve to educate and invite readers to think about their own assumptions, attitudes, and behaviors when playing or working with someone who has a disability. If readers dig into a text and have opportunities to share their responses with others, they will, it is hoped, be conscious of not doing that "look-away thing" when encountering someone who is differently abled.

Personal Stories about Ableism

John Myers has been teacher, consultant, and university instructor for more than 40 years. He is an expert in the field of Social Studies and History curricula.

Let's start with SHAME!

I felt shame at being visually impaired and diagnosed as such as an infant to the point that there was a question as to whether I could go to regular school. Even sitting at the front of the class was no guarantee that I could read what was on the chalkboard or a PowerPoint slide. Shame at having up and down moods. Shame at having such pale, sensitive skin that walking in the sunshine—even for periods as short as recess—is a recipe for severe burns, as happened in my early school days.

How many students hide their perceived weakness out of a sense of shame or because they feel they are, as in the title of the play and movie, "Children of a Lesser God"? I suppose my shame was, alas, a kind of self-hate. When meeting others who might turn away from me, tease me, or exclude me, I wonder about where their prejudice and shameful attitude comes from, a discrimination and hate that others might project on people like me just because we were born a little different.
— John Myers

Traveling alone as a person with low vision is an act of pride and an expression of freedom. Especially when traveling abroad, travelling alone was an act that gave me the belief that I was invincible—I could do it all, go anywhere, overcome all obstacles as a person with a disability. More often than not, this pride created more danger and humor than it was intended to avoid. I had also absorbed the negative influence of ableism—that I was some kind of an Avenger or superhuman who was able to mask physical disability with superhuman abilities. It was a pride that would thrust me into unknown international territory without a cane, a guide, or a comrade to support me. I refused help and any assistive device that identified me as having low vision. I wanted to make my disability invisible because I thought that passing for fully sighted was worth more than my personal safety or benefit.

Growing up, I never used a cane. In hindsight, It would have improved my life in my earlier years in many ways, allowing me to access my world using intuitive senses. It wasn't until I had an accident in Israel in 2008 that I realized that there is no shame in embracing technology and devices that help me. I was hiking between cities with a student group when my foot slipped on a rocky part of the path beneath me. I fell down the edge of a path elevated on the side of a mountain. It was a fall that could have been avoided. It also could have been much worse. The use of a cane extended a few paces before me allows me to anticipate my next moves before making them. It would have been able to help me determine where safe ground was located. I was more concerned with making what made me different invisible. Thankfully, by the grace of luck, I landed safely on a rocky ledge below that overlooked the mountain. I no longer fear being seen with my cane because I know that it keeps me safe and allows me to navigate the world safely. Embracing my cane allowed me to expand my mobility and gain deeper access to the places I visit. I learned to love the tool that I used to push away because it allows me to be fully present where I am and connected to my surroundings.

— Theodore Walker Robinson

Bookshelf: Picture Books Featuring Physical Challenges
Arnie and the New Kid by Nancy Carlson
The Black Book of Colors by Menena Cottin; illus. Rosana Faria
Don't Call Me Special: A First Look at Disability by Pat Thomas
Six Dots: A Story of Young Louis Braille by Jennifer Bryant; illus. Boris Kulikov
Seven Blind Mice by Ed Young
Susan Laughs by Jeanne Willis; illus. Tony Ross

3

Dismantling Hate in Schools

"Smile more than you cry, give more than you take, and love more than you hate."
— Drake, singer

"Although we live in a world that is still fraught with hatred, fear and bullying, we have the capacity both individually and collectively to create change and to embody values that make the world a safer place for everyone, regardless of how we look or who we love."
— Marcel d'Entremont, performer

Hate in Schools

Text on pages 51–56 was written by Kaschka Watson and Andrew Campbell.

Our schools are becoming more unsafe for students due to rampant incidents of racism and other forms of discrimination that are leveled against students who identify as Black, Indigenous, racialized, or 2SLGBTQIA+, as well as students with disabilities and those who are "othered."

The CBC News (2021) outlines some examples of how students are experiencing racism, discrimination and hate in classrooms.

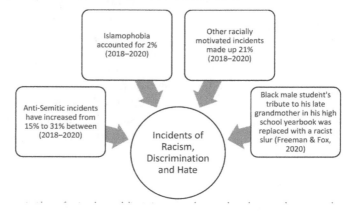

These incidents of racism, hate, and discriminatory attacks on students that are underrepresented come as no surprise to the students and their parents who are affected. In fact, students and their parents have been complaining about these disparities for years, despite numerous equity and inclusion policies that have been implemented to help dismantle racism, hate, and discrimination in our schools. These negative experiences shape students' educational experiences and lead to feelings of isolation, degradation, psychological violence, and harm (Maynard, 2022). Classroom teachers have a responsibility, now more than ever, to ensure that they are deliberate and intentional in their pedagogy in erasing hate through anti-discriminatory practices.

PERSPECTIVE

Planning Pedagogy Using an Anti-Discrimination Lens

by Kaschka Watson

Dr. Kaschka Watson is a graduate of the Ontario Institute for Studies in Education at the University of Toronto. His research interests include racial and ethnic relations, inclusive leadership and policy, diversity and leadership, social justice and equity, student engagement, and underrepresented faculty in higher education.

See page 136 for references and resources.

The planning of pedagogy through an anti-discriminatory lens calls on classroom teachers, educators, and practitioners to be creative, intentional, deliberate, open-minded, strategic, flexible, and inclusive in their instruction. This means that the ways in which educators think about and plan their pedagogy must centre around, but not be limited to, the following key principles:

- Examination of conscious and unconscious biases
- Evaluating the impact of power and privilege
- Amplifying marginalized students' voices
- Critically analyzing historical context
- Supporting students' health and well-being
- Holding high expectations of marginalized students (Murray et al., 2020)

Conscious and Unconscious Biases

Educators who are committed to making anti-racist changes to their teaching need to be aware of their own conscious and unconscious biases. Self-examination challenges educators to consider their own biases, and requires them to think about the diverse backgrounds and communities of their students, the discriminatory issues marginalized students face, and how racism, discrimination, and hate have impact on marginalized students' experiences and their academic success. Educators who engage in self-examination of their biases, assumptions, and experiences can help to identify and eliminate discriminatory ideas that can have negative impacts on students' academic experience (Murray et al., 2020) and to determine what actions must be taken to eliminate discrimination in their schools (Campbell & Watson, 2021). Begin by asking yourself these questions:

1. What biases do I hold that are most likely to affect my behavior and what proactive steps can I take to reduce their impact?
2. How am I making space for marginalized students' experiences in my teaching and assessment techniques?
3. How can I diversify and make the curriculum more inclusive to help dismantle and eliminate stereotypes?
4. What steps am I taking to understand the significance of embedding anti-discriminatory practices in my pedagogy?

The Impact of Power and Privilege

Educators who evaluate their power and privilege are better able to create inclusive and safe learning spaces, and instructional activities that foster students' diverse experiences (Lopez, 2013). Here are a few suggestions for teaching with an anti-discriminatory lens.

Evaluating Power	Evaluating Privilege
Examine the textbooks being used and your approach to teaching	Reflect on your privileges and how they inform your biases
Be intentional about the instructional materials and assessment practices used	Determine which students get access to certain resources/instructional materials
Consider how you interact with all students, and whose knowledge is being valued and included	Challenging the dominant stories being told as part of the pedagogy
Be purposeful in the connections being made with students, parents, and their community	Build a social network and be mindful of how diverse and inclusive the members are
Recognize the importance of creating positive classroom learning spaces for all students (Lopez, 2013)	Make room for diverse experiences in the learning process

Amplifying Students' Voices

One way of ensuring that marginalized students feel valued and welcomed in the classroom is to provide the opportunity for their voices to be reflected through pedagogical practices. Educators must take the histories and lived experiences of marginalized students into their planning. For example, students need to feel connected to the school culture and to the curriculum; they must see themselves represented in educators' teaching practice (Campbell & Watson, 2021). Many of our students are disengaged in the classroom because educators have not found ways to incorporate students' voices in the activities and methods of instruction being administered. Amplifying students' voices means that educators will have to

- Listen: Truly listen and understand marginalized students' experiences and not interject their own
- React: Be intentionally anti-racist and challenge power structures and policies that mute students' voices in the curriculum
- Support: Acknowledge the ways anti-racism is evident in the classroom; provide students with the tools/resources they need to amplify their voices.

Not all students' voices are being heard, so deliberate actions are needed to ensure that students' voices are a part of achieving equity in our education system (Campbell & Watson, 2021b). Students need to feel safe to participate in their learning. For example, educators can incorporate resources in their pedagogy that initiate culturally relevant conversations and encourage students to share their experiences (Murray et al., 2020). The planning and delivery of instruction have to empower students to speak up and be engaged in the classroom, which is possible only if they know their voices matter and they have been given the opportunity to express themselves freely.

Historical Context
Shields et al (2005) articulated that educators should know that the emergence of the pathologizing of the lived experiences of racially marginalized students has its basis in colonial and imperial history. According to Milner and Smithey (2003), educators who have a great awareness of students' diversity and the historical impact of systemic barriers on their educational experiences are best able to disrupt and dismantle deficit thinking towards marginalized students. To maximize marginalized students' learning opportunities, educators must know the experiences and cultural differences of the students they serve and translate the knowledge of marginalized students' histories into instructional practices that are not discriminatory.

Student Mental Health and Well-Being
The mental health and well-being of students play a crucial role in their engagement and educational experiences at schools and in classrooms. Schmidt (2020) argued that students see their school experience as a culture that makes them feel good in their own skin and not feel stressful. Students want their schools and classrooms to be a place that is supportive, inspiring, diverse, and inclusive. However, many marginalized students do not feel like they can turn to educators when they need help. As a result, they feel less positive about themselves and they experience anxiety, loneliness, and low self-confidence (Yau et al., 2015). Educators are encouraged to examine the ways in which their pedagogical planning is making room for marginalized students' mental health and well-being, and how activities and assessments can positively or negatively affect students' educational experience.

Holding High Expectations of Marginalized Students
When educators plan their pedagogy through an anti-discriminatory lens, it means that they hold high expectations of all their students, regardless of their diverse backgrounds. Holding high expectations of marginalized students is believing in their success (Yau et al., 2015). Educators should focus on marginalized students' creativity and growth, and not assume that they do not need support to be successful in the classroom. As educators plan their pedagogy, they are looking at the different ways they can help students to be more engaged in their learning, and seeing the value of their differences and how those differences can add value to the curriculum and pedagogy (Portelli, 2010).

Intersecting Identities

> "Intersectionality is a lens through which you can see where power comes and collides, where it locks and intersects. It is the acknowledgement that everyone has their own unique experiences of discrimination and privilege."
> — Kimberlé Crenshaw

Many schools are diverse, and students come to the classrooms with their unique intersecting identities. Students' race, sexual preferences, religious beliefs, gender identities, and socio-economic statuses are dimensions of their identities that make them who they are (Swartz, 2020). Because of this, many of them have faced and continue to face barriers because of their intersectionality.

It is crucial that the differences and unique identities of all students are taken into consideration to effectively address the vulnerabilities of students that "reflect the intersections of racism, sexism, class oppression, transphobia, able-ism and more" (Henry et al., 2017, p. 16). Educators are in a unique position to be aware of the challenges and the hate that marginalized students are facing because of their multiple identities. Therefore, it is important for educators to talk more about students' intersectionality and how a lack of awareness and knowledge of intersectionality can affect students' educational experiences and outcomes.

Personal Stories

In the 1970s, my mother immigrated to Toronto, Ontario, from her native country Somalia. She found residence in the Black Creek region of North York, an area known for the lack of social resources and a social stigma, as it had a growing racialized population. My experiences in education are greatly shaped by the way I was perceived by peers and educators.

Growing up, I was always either perceived as Muslim or Black, never both. I was never allowed the space to be fully seen as a Black Muslim girl. As I started to wear the hijab at a young age, it would always be the first marker to indicate my difference. Most of my peers were either Black or non-white, so my true difference to them was my hijab. I would receive comments about it from everyone, and educators were no exception.

The starkest comment I can remember is one from a Black female teacher, who made a comment about my sweater. It was during the spring, and she was shocked I was wearing a long-sleeve sweater. She explained that she could never cover up like me, because she loves to show off her arms. She then questioned if I was "hot in that," referring to my hijab. I was taken aback and wanted to reply that, of course not, I feel just the way you feel. Normal!

One would think that being Black, Muslim, and a woman would award me with more people to feel belonging with, but I felt more ostracized. This created a push-pull factor with my identities. I would go back and forth, between feeling more aligned with either identity. I often felt like I could only show fragments of myself to be accepted. It was only when I was in spaces with other Black Muslim girls that I felt whole. During my entire childhood, many of my friendships were with other Black Muslim girls. I write this to say that the Black experience in education is not all universal. Our community building should be based on the celebration of our differences, not the similarities.

— Halima D.

My champion was Ms. Matthews. She was one of the women who had a significant impact on me and inspired me to pursue teaching. She was also the *first* black female teacher I ever had. Ms. Matthews, my Grade 5 teacher, was the first person who ever told me I was Black. It never dawned on me that I was Black because I really had no concept of race at the time. This opened up a completely new world for me when it came to my identity. I knew I was Somali, and I knew I was Muslim, but I never realized I was *Black*. My parents, coming from a fairly homogeneous nation (Somalia), were never really cognizant of the nuances of race. Everyone they knew looked like them in Somalia, they were all one race. Ms. Matthews taught me so much about the history of Africa and explained to me how and why I was Black and what it meant. She made me realize that there was a collective group of people with which I shared similar experiences. All I wanted as a I kid was to belong, and Ms. Matthews made me feel like I did. I was diagnosed with Type 1 diabetes at the age of 10 and my parents were too afraid to let me go out for recess and play, for fear that I would go hypoglycemic. I spent my lunches with Ms. Matthews, listening to reggae music and watching her run her steelpan club. I learned so much from her and I am so grateful to have met her. I am grateful for her taking the opportunity to teach me about the concept of race when I was at such a young age because it triggered immense growth and learning in the years to come.
— Magda A.

Lesson: Exploring Intersectionality

1. Invite students to create an example of intersectionality using four (4) or more multiple identities.
2. Ask students to give two or more examples of how people might be affected by intersectionality.

Disrupting Deficit Thinking

> "When given the choice between right or being kind, choose kind."
> — Mr. Browne's September precept, *Wonder* by R.J. Palacio, p. 48

When you hear the term *deficit thinking*, what comes to your mind? Your definition might include weakness, a focus on the negative, or a singular story that does not account for all factors and perspectives. Throughout classrooms and broader society, many indicators exist to tell students they do not belong. Without a sense of safety and belonging in schools, students' learning and growth will likely suffer negative impacts. This is deficit thinking. Deficit thinking over-simplifies students' vast and heterogenous experiences by focusing on their perceived shortcomings rather than strengths (Porter et al., 2021). Students do not come to school empty; students come with cultural awareness of self and others. How can we take what students bring to our classroom communities, use it, build it, expand upon it, and add to it? How can we improve our toolboxes to shift from deficit thinking to asset- and strength-based approaches?

Deficit thinking is rooted in victim blaming, suggesting that people are responsible for their predicaments and failing to acknowledge that they live in coercive systems that cause harm without accountability. Are we teaching in a singular way, where everybody is getting the same portion and being addressed without recognition of their unique contexts? Are we taking universal design for learning, differentiated learning, and accommodations into consideration? We need to move past the issues that students bring with them in their invisible backpacks. If a student is homeless, how do we consider equity rather than deficit? Can the homework be adjusted, can the student come to school early to use a computer lab, can we create access in unique and personal ways for this student? We must work intentionally to make sure that all our students have the opportunity to thrive and be successful. If we dig deeper and move past the deficits, we can find pedagogies and strength-based approaches that really are inclusive for all.

In order to confront perceptions of deficit mentalities, it is essential that we move to strength-based approaches. In doing so, we are ensuring that our pedagogy and our practice are culturally relevant and responsive. Otherwise, educators can easily allow their deficit thinking and deficit pedagogy to result in the underachievement of students and to further reinforce the stereotypes about marginalized students' ability and success in schools (McMahan & Portelli, 2012). As educators, the choices and mentalities we hold can have a life-altering impact on students both within and beyond our classroom, shaping their lifestyles and opportunities well into post-secondary pursuits and lifelong learning (Smit, 2012).

PERSPECTIVE

Two Stories of Disruption

by Andrew Campbell

When I was a young teacher, I gave my Grade 5 students a typical exercise at the start of the school year: to write a story about how they spent their summer. As I read their responses, I remember being shocked to see students lying in their stories. Why did they do that? Because of the messaging in the classroom. The message our schools were sending was one of privilege: where did you go for summer, where did you travel, what exciting things did you do that were worthy of summer? I saw my students writing that they went to Disneyland, a cottage, Canada's Wonderland, and so many other exciting places that aligned with the messages to which our school and society insisted they conform. Very early on, these students were understanding that the only thing that really mattered about their time away was the exciting ways they spent their summer. If someone went to see their grandmother in the country and helped to pick coffee or take care of the animals, that wasn't considered essay-worthy. I realized that I needed to make a change so that all student backgrounds were supported, listened to, and validated (Campbell, 2022a). This experience helped me to realize that we must be careful of how we allow our students to share who they are, their lives, and their stories. Are we creating space for all stories and all our students' lived experiences, or only those that match our visions of an exciting summer? Are we not just creating the space, but valuing that space? How can we do better?

At another school, the students had a snack program. This was presented as a deficit scenario: the snack program was for the kids who needed a snack because they didn't have sufficient resources from home. Children were called down on the intercom system to line up at a certain window and sit in a certain room. Suddenly, everyone could see that these were the kids in need, the kids who didn't have enough. A program that was intended to help our students served to further marginalize them and take away their dignity.

The principal decided to make a change. The snack bin would be placed in an area of the school that every single person had access to. The snack bin was no longer for those who were hungry or didn't have a snack or couldn't afford snacks; it was for anyone who wanted one. Teachers, students, staff, administrators, or anyone else who wanted a snack could have one, making it less of a target for stereotyping. Students could see teachers walking by and taking something, so that they didn't feel like they were taking a snack only because they were poor and doing without. To take it a step further, the school implemented an option for people to put snacks into the bin and help one another. This simple action and consideration transformed a situation from deficit to growth. (Campbell, 2022b)

Taking Action Against Deficit Thinking

As Educators

What critical questions can we ask ourselves, the system, the class, and the school about how deficit thinking is perpetuated? Can it be found in schools, activities, sports, books, morning announcements, report-card writing? The language we use in schools can further oppress certain students. Are we blaming our students and their families for things over which they have no control? What are your students coming to school with? We see their backpacks filled with pencils, crayons, and books. Do we also see the students coming to school with mental-health issues, homelessness, poverty, and trauma?

Deficit thinking implies that lives that differ from the norm are deprived, negative, and disadvantaged. It is important that we see all students as students: amazing, full of dreams, and with infinite possibilities. When we see our students in this way, our job is to figure out how to maintain, hold, and support our expectations to disrupt systems within and outside of our schools that affect all students' success. When we see a student as only a laundry list of problems, we are then unable to look beyond the student's more challenging behavior to foster meaningful and reciprocal relationships. To disrupt deficit thinking, anti-Black racism, Islamophobia, homophobia, and all the other methods of oppression in schools, it is vital that we take the time to focus on relationships. We must engage in a positive relationship with our students and see them as more than just numbers and a checkbox. We need to connect to their lived experiences and ensure that our pedagogy and practice are culturally relevant and responsive.

Pause and Reflect for Educators

1. What specific situations have you seen in your school that prompted deficit thinking in yourself? In your students?
2. How could you approach the situation from a strength-based mindset?
3. What can you alter about your classroom culture to foster an environment where all students are seen for their unique strengths?
4. What deficit narratives do you tell yourself that shape the way you teach and lead?

For Students

As educators, one of the most powerful ways we can disrupt deficit thinking is by encouraging our students to take action. The following list outlines several possibilities for fostering a culture of equity and deficit disruption in the classroom.

1. Promote student voice by co-constructing and collaborating on assignments, rubrics, and lesson planning to ensure that all students are supported. Students must be encouraged and supported in this endeavor through active listening and genuine consideration of their input and ideas.
2. Uphold democratic principles when curating class content by brainstorming as a class, shortlisting ideas, and allowing the entire class to vote on ideas that work best for all students. To further support culturally relevant and responsive pedagogy, students may be invited to share the rationale behind their vote.
3. Educate students about how deficit thinking leads to stereotyping and prejudging of marginalized people based on misinformation or misconstructions, leaving no place for it in the classroom (Sharma, 2016).
4. Encourage students to question deficit attitudes they encounter and to disrupt deficit behaviors when they see them.
5. Invite students to celebrate and showcase differences, sustaining a classroom culture in which there is no tolerance for hate, prejudice, and discrimination.
6. Students may also be asked to think critically about disrupting deficits in classroom discussions and activities, such as considering such questions as

   - Have you ever made a negative judgment about someone else before getting to know them?
   - Why do you think this happened, and what did you do about it?
   - What strategies can we use to expose ourselves to more difference and to celebrate the differences in our lives, both at school and at home?
   - Imagine a scenario where a friend is struggling. What actions can you take to remind your friend of their strengths? How can you collaboratively problem-solve so that everybody wins?

Lesson: What Would You Do?

The What Would You Do? reproducible on pages 61–62 presents incidents of intolerance, discrimination, and hate, as well as alternatives for dealing with them. There might not be an easy answer to each event; however, through discussion, students can consider the challenges, the pros and cons of putting each of the choices into action.

1. Students study the scenarios independently and then share their responses in small groups.
2. After working in small groups, have a whole-class discussion:
   - Which of these scenarios was the most challenging to consider?
   - Which of these scenarios reminded students of incidents from their own lives or someone they know?
   - In some cases, what might a fourth alternative course of action be?

Lesson: What If…?

What If? scenarios on the reproducible on page 63 can be explored using these strategies. Some students might wish to suggest an alternative action.

Whole-class Discussion

To begin, offer a single scenario to the whole class for discussion. Some students may choose to reveal similar incidents that have happened to them or someone they know. As the discussion continues, have students offer suggestions about how to handle the situation in the present and for the future.

Independent Response, Then Small-group Discussion

Distribute the reproducible to the class. Students review the list and choose one situation to focus on. In answer to their chosen What If...? question, they can write a possible solution to the problem, then meet with at least two others who have chosen a different scenario to discuss ways to take action.

Random Selection

Cut What If...? statements into strips and place in an envelope. Students working in pairs or groups of three randomly select one item from the envelope to discuss. Challenge students to list three optional solutions to the problem. Students then work with another group to share their responses.

Role-playing

Students form groups of two or three. Each group is assigned a scenario from the list, and group members discuss the incident and possible solutions. They collaborate to prepare an improvised scene that tells a story of discrimination and how it was solved. Once students have rehearsed their improvisation, they can present it to another group.

What Would You Do?

1. You received an email with the message *I HATE YOU*. You don't know who the sender is. You would…
   a) Delete and ignore the message.
   b) Reply to the message with a warning that you are reporting the incident.
   c) Report the message to an adult right away.

2. You're having lunch with friends at school. When one of your friends opens their lunch, someone calls out, "Oooo, that's so gross!" You would…
   a) Offer some of your own lunch to your friend.
   b) Insult the attacker for the lunch they brought.
   c) Ask your friend if you could try some of their lunch.

3. A friend has told you that she was bullied and harassed for wearing a hijab. She doesn't want to tell her parents because she's afraid that they might worry. You would…
   a) Advise your friend that she needs to talk to a parent and ask them to intervene.
   b) Offer to talk to the bully (with or without your friend).
   c) Tell someone else you know about the incident because you don't know how to handle it.

4. You are visiting a daycare centre. You notice that a boy is being teased because he is wearing a dress in the dress-up centre. You hear two girls tell him, "Boys don't wear dresses." You would…
   a) Encourage the girls to try on different clothes and join the boy.
   b) Have a conversation with the two girls and explain that it's okay if the boy wants to wear a dress during playtime.
   c) Compliment the boy on his dress and tell him to ignore the girls.

5. You're walking with friends down the hall at school. After passing by two other boys, you hear them call out, "Fag." You would…
   a) Turn and confront the boys.
   b) Ignore the comment. It's a common put-down and you can't change the boys.
   c) Talk with your friends and plan a way to get back at the boys.

6. You hear a good friend calling someone you don't know a bad name. You would…
   a) Try not to get involved.
   b) Ask your friend why they enjoy making someone feel bad.
   c) Call your friend a bad name, then ask, "How do you feel?"

Pembroke Publishers ©2023 *Stop the Hate for Goodness Sake* by Andrew Campbell and Larry Swartz ISBN 958-1-55138-358-3

What Would You Do? (cont'd)

7. You have a new neighbor that you've become friends with. Your old friends make fun of them because the clothes they wear are badly torn and somewhat smelly. You would…
    a) Tell your old friends that they are being mean and should stop.
    b) Advise your neighbor to get some new clothes and offer to help.
    c) Invite your old friends over to your house to have fun with the new neighbor.

8. Josh is known to be the class clown. When a new student in the class walks by his desk, Josh says, "Why don't you go back where you came from?" When he realizes people are noticing, Josh says, "I was just joking!" You would….
    a) Challenge Josh about his harmful comment.
    b) Have a conversation with the new student, assuring them that not everyone is like Josh.
    c) Have a conversation with Josh and the new student together.

9. Someone left a hateful message inside your desk. This isn't the first time. The teacher is aware there may be a problem in the class but hasn't done anything about it. You would…
    a) Show the teacher the message and let them handle it.
    b) Show the note to your parents and ask them connect with the teacher to address the situation.
    c) Ignore it. It's not worth it.

10. You are in the change room after a gym class. Some of your classmates are talking about how overweight another classmate is. You would:
    a) Ignore your classmates because the student didn't know they were being talked about. No harm done.
    b) Tell the gym teacher what you heard in the change room.
    c) Befriend the person who was being talked about and assure them that they should be comfortable with who they are.

Pembroke Publishers ©2023 *Stop the Hate for Goodness Sake* by Andrew Campbell and Larry Swartz ISBN 958-1-55138-358-3

What If…?

As you read each of these true-to-life incidents of hate, think about what you would do or say to address/confront the incident. Which scenario is the most challenging for you to consider? Which scenario reminds you of incidents from your own life, or the life of someone you know?

1. *What if…* you are walking home from school and you see someone spray-painting a piece of graffiti that could be consider offensive to you or someone you know?

2. *What if…* you receive an email that says something racist about one of your best friends and that friend is unaware of the email?

3. *What if…* you are in a store with your friends and you overhear a customer making fun of the cashier's accent?

4. *What if…* someone in your school calls out a homophobic slur every time they pass you in the hallway, and you hear giggling as they walk away?

5. *What if…* a student in your class uses a wheelchair and they are often excluded from participating in gym class or other class events?

6. *What if…* your cousin tells you he was bullied at school because he wore nail polish?

7. *What if…* you saw someone in the washroom who was really upset because someone made fun of the lunch they were eating and, when you volunteer to help, the person refuses?

8. *What if…* you arrive at school and notice that someone painted a swastika on a locker near yours?

9. *What if…* an immigrant family moves into your neighborhood. Neighbors put up a sign on their own front lawn saying, "*Go home!*"?

10. *What if…* you hear someone telling a racist joke?

11. *What if…* you are on the school bus and you witness someone making fun of a girl wearing a hijab?

12. *What if…* your best friend tells you that someone made fun of their skin color, and their parent advised them to ignore such incidents because reacting to it will only lead to more trouble?

13. *What if…* your father comes to pick you up at school wearing a pink shirt and some classmates make fun of this?

14. *What if…* the teacher's back is turned and you witness someone in your class mocking the teacher's religion? Their weight?

15. *What if…* you are having lunch with friends and hear someone at the next table say, "I'm so tired of hearing 'Black Lives Matter'. All lives matter."?

16. *What If…* you invite a friend over for a family celebration and you hear some say, "She's pretty for a fat girl/Asian girl/Black girl/disabled person."?

17. *What if…* you hear someone say, "I'm not racist!"?

Pembroke Publishers ©2023 *Stop the Hate for Goodness Sake* by Andrew Campbell and Larry Swartz ISBN 958-1-55138-358-3

4

Ways to Erase Hate

"Taking chances means carrying hope in your heart, for the possible and impossible dreams. But it goes beyond that—hope is nothing without luck, mentorship, support, cheerleaders and a lot of hard work."
— Uzma Jalaluddin, columnist, *Toronto Star*, March 2, 2022

Embrace Diversity

Take a moment to look around your classroom and notice how difference surrounds you, and the many opportunities we have to love and celebrate our differences. Each educator and student is a different person, with a unique ethnicity, race, religion, family structure, and identity. School should be a place of love, kindness, celebration, and learning about these differences, with no place or space for hate. As educators, it is crucial that we cultivate and foster educational spaces that actively dismantle racism through raising awareness, upholding standards of equity, and taking action.

Identity

Our classrooms, like our lives, need to be about building better relationships. An important place to start is to have students think about their identities and to learn about the identities of others they work and play with each day. *Identity* is the word we use to talk about who we are as a person. What makes me *me*, and you *you*, is the stuff of our identity. In *The Antiracist Kid* Tiffany Jewell writes: "Everyone has an identity. No other person in the world has the same identity as you."

Personal identity is what makes each person different from other people. When thinking about our personal identities, it is important to consider our names, ages, homes, preferences in food and culture, hobbies, talents and interests, and the people we care about and love. Personal identity comes from
- family
- community
- experiences

Social identity is the part of our identity that relates to other people in the community and around the world. Social identities fit into categories that have been named, created, and defined by society; for example,
- race
- ethnicity
- gender
- sexual identity
- religion
- citizenship
- class

Racial identity refers to what other people see when they look at your skin color, hair texture, and other parts of the way you look. People who look similar in these ways are part of the same group, even if not part of the same family. That group is called a *race*. In North America, the larger groups of race used by governments often include (but are not limited to) categories like these:
- Black/Afro-American
- Indigenous/Native American
- Asian: East Asian, South Asian, etc.
- Latino/Latinx/Hispanic
- White

PERSPECTIVE

Combatting Inequality and Supporting Jewish Identity

by Karen R. Mock

The goal of inclusive education and quest for equity and justice involves us in the struggle against all forms of racism and bigotry, and the obligation and responsibility to promote human rights for all our students and colleagues. However, a necessary first step in achieving human rights for all is for educators to become aware of and come to terms with the extent of all forms of discrimination and the promotion of hatred in this country. Only through

Dr. Karen Mock is a human-rights consultant, educational psychologist, certified teacher, and teacher educator. She is former Executive Director of the Canadian Race Relations Foundation and of the League for Human Rights of B'nai Brith Canada, and is qualified by Canadian courts and human rights tribunals as an expert on human rights, discrimination, racism, antisemitism, hate crime, and hate-group activity.

Although this essay is about antisemitism in particular, its lessons apply to erasing hate of all kinds.

See page 137 for references and resources.

awareness and acceptance of the realities will we be able to mobilize the energy and resources necessary for the remedies.

While anti-racism/anti-oppression have become the norm in schools today, as well as in teacher education faculties, sadly it has been my experience that the topic of antisemitism, known as the longest hatred, has been omitted from the social justice curriculum. Here are 10 things I believe educators need to know and do about antisemitism:

1. Understand and Recognize Antisemitic Propaganda
The goal of hate propaganda and hate mongers is to portray a group as inferior, even less than human, undermining the norms and values of a society by potentially taking control of the culture through power or sheer numbers. The targets of hatred are the objects of prejudice and stereotyping, often characterized as taking advantage of the rest of society and a threat that ought to be removed. People are most receptive to hate mongering when they are looking for someone to blame for their problems so that they can feel better about themselves. Difficult economic times or disasters or pandemics inevitably lead to this pattern of scapegoating, and any identifiable minority group is at risk.

Another goal of hate mongers is to instill fear or terror in their victims. Attacks are often particularly vicious, leaving entire communities feeling vulnerable and isolated. Hate can lead to group members experiencing a negative self-image, self-doubt, and a feeling of worthlessness. Individuals may try to assimilate or disappear as an identifiable group, but hate mongers would suggest that this is impossible. According to avowed racists and white supremacists, the minority traits remain as a contaminant of the society or pure race, and must therefore be eliminated to whatever extent possible.

2. Know that Hate Speech is Not a Free-Speech Issue
Even when the audience is unreceptive, hate propaganda can do damage in that it plays on people's doubts and fears, and feeds on misconceptions, increasing barriers to understanding. Hate propaganda contributes to disunity in society, compromises democratic values, and maintains inequality and oppression. It is ironic that white supremacists and hate mongers are among the most outspoken advocates of free speech, when they use that freedom to deny others their freedoms. The Holocaust did not start with guns and gas chambers—it started with words. Canada learned this lesson of the Holocaust, so that in this country hate propaganda is not a free-speech issue. It is the promotion of hatred against an identifiable group, and in Canada it is against the law.

3. Know Both History and the Present
It has been well-documented that racism against racialized communities has long been part of the Canadian experience, in particular against Indigenous and Black Canadians. But there is also evidence of rampant antisemitism in the early days of Canada. However, as the recent City of Toronto campaign against antisemitism in their *Toronto For All* program has so clearly illustrated, antisemitism is not a thing of the past. As Santayana put it, "Those who do not know history are doomed to repeat it."

4. Validate Identities

An important way to counter antisemitism is to ensure that students and teachers also know about the positive history of Jews in Canada and their significant contributions to society, not just the destruction of most European Jews in the Holocaust. There are three components of Jewish identities: Jewish *peoplehood* (an ethnic identity or nationhood, binding Jews worldwide); the Jewish *religion* (observance of spiritual and ritual tenets of Judaism, with various denominations within the faith: e.g., Orthodox, Conservative, Reform, Reconstructionist, Humanistic); and Jewish *culture* (celebration of traditions, both secular and religious, and foods!). Jewish traditions can vary culturally depending on country of origin of the family or ancestors. It is important also to acknowledge that there are not only Jews of European descent (Ashkenazi) who are primarily white, but there are also many Jews of color (Sephardic, Latino, Black/African, Asian, and South Asian, as well as Misrachi Jews from Arab lands). Celebrate Jewish holidays and festivals in your schools and classrooms in ways that are authentic.

5. Name and Call Out All Incidents of Hate

All educators and administrators need to know what to do when it comes to implementation of the principles of multiculturalism, equity, and social justice...*and* human rights, anti-racism, and anti-oppression principles, *and* safe schools and anti-hate principles and laws. Put into practice the skills of empathy and active listening. Ensure that the victim is supported, and that there are consequences and counselling for the perpetrators. Bystanders, too, need to know how the incident was handled. Don't hide behind claims of confidentiality. There are ways to debrief bystanders without violating privacy. Most students and staff suffer in silence and don't report incidents. They think nothing will be done because they never hear how incidents were resolved.

6. Recognize that Systemic Problems Require Systemic Solutions

Even in 2022, there were many reported incidents of schools holding events important to Jewish students and staff on Jewish holy days, clearly against Board and Ministry policy. Every school should have the Multifaith Calendar. Are you commemorating days of significance in an equitable manner, and not in a discriminatory manner? Our work in equity is about systemic change, such that all students see themselves reflected. It is important to include the local community as a partner, and to communicate effectively and regularly to enhance community relations with the administration and staff, and between and among the diverse communities you serve. In schools and workplaces, ensure all the following systemic issues are considered to prevent antisemitism (and every other –ism and phobia):

- Formal curriculum (At every level of the system, who is represented and who is not?)
- Hidden curriculum (the informal environment in the school. Does it prioritize some groups over others? Are there triggering issues or representations?)
- Holiday celebrations (When? What? Whose?)
- Possibly political agenda (Is the curriculum factual or biased in terms of political propaganda? Is the student required to adhere to the teacher's bias?)

7. Understand the Impact of Trauma on Victims of Oppression and Hate

It is very important for those who have not experienced racism or other forms of oppression to understand why incidents that might seem trivial can be painful to members of racialized or minority groups, depending on their level of trauma, and the triggering event(s). Trauma can be transferred through historical trauma, genetics, and even changes in DNA, passed on from generation to generation as narrative and by modelling. It results in feelings of powerlessness and often has social and economic impact that continues to affect behavior and mental health. Defeat has greater impact than victory on the psyche and also fuels ethnic nationalism for centuries. It is for this reason that a slogan at a demonstration may be innocuous to some and interpreted to be a simple call for freedom, but can be the foreboding cry of a genocidal threat to Jewish observers.

8. Question if Your Demographic Data Is Accurate or Exclusive

Many student and staff surveys ask people to self-identify as Racialized or White; African, Caribbean, Black Community, Indigenous, Asian, LGBTQ2, etc. Who is "othered"? Where and how do Jewish students and staff locate themselves when excluded from the surveys? That is, unless religion and ethnicity are categories, what do Jewish people do as a historically and currently "racialized" community when the only choice they have is to check off *white*? All schools need to ensure that their school climate and their assessment tools and surveys are truly inclusive and validate all students' identities.

9. Know that Jewish People Are Not White Supremacists

There is a trend for many anti-racist educators to insist that all white people, including Jews, are to be labelled "white supremacists" and even to go so far as to ask them to self-identify as such. While it is important for white people in a white-dominated society to understand white privilege, to use the term *white supremacists* in this case is to co-opt and change the meaning of the term. Terms like *apartheid*, *genocide*, *Holocaust*, and *white supremacy* have been coopted and the meaning appropriated to express the pain and suffering some groups experience. School officials must ensure that anti-oppression theories and practices are not used to oppress others, and that victims do not become victimizers. We need also to ensure we do not have a double standard when it comes to Jews. It is a norm of anti-racism work that groups can define their own oppression. They certainly know both what it looks like and how it feels. It is the same for Jews and antisemitism.

10. Ensure Equity and Inclusive Education Teams Are Truly Inclusive

Where are non-Jewish students, staff, and colleagues in the discussion of antisemitism? Where and to whom do Jewish students and staff go when they are victims of antisemitism and need help? In many schools and boards, Jewish members of the school community (students, staff, parents) feel they have nowhere to turn to resolve the tensions they are experiencing. Their experiences in the system have forced them to turn to the outside for help. Is there support within your school and/or board for victims of antisemitism? Is there effective education and training of board personnel on the subject?

Unfortunately, rather than ensuring preventative measures are in place through curriculum and pro-active programming, many administrations do not take action against antisemitism until there is a complaint from a parent or the community. There is no question it is far better for school–community relations to be proactive than reactive.

In conclusion, I believe that three questions of the great Hebrew sage Hillel summarize our important work in human rights, anti-racism, equity, and inclusion…including our ongoing struggle against antisemitism:

> If I am not for myself, who will be for me?
> But if I am only for myself, what am I?
> If not now, when?

Lesson: My Identity

In this lesson, students are invited to think about words that would best describe them and consider how these words are part of our identities.

My Identity in Words

1. Have students answer the following question: *What are five or six words you would use to describe yourself to someone who doesn't know you?*
2. Have students review the words and determine which are related to physical description, which are related to their personalities, and which are related to their culture.

Identity Word Cloud

A word cloud is a useful medium in which students collect and present words that are connected to their identities.

1. The list of words from My Identity in Words can be used as a start.
2. Students add other words that list their interests, hobbies, and talents; words to describe their personalities, relationships, etc.
3. Use an online program to generate word clouds from text that students provide. The clouds give greater prominence to words that appear frequently in the source text. Students can tweak word clouds with different fonts, layouts, and color schemes.
4. Once completed, students can print a copy of their word cloud and share it with others by discussing
   - why they chose the words they did to represent their identities
   - which words stand out in the design; which are repeated
   - which words are their favorites; which words they might choose to add
   - how they might alter the design of the word cloud they created

Extension: Identity List Poem

List poems follow a syntactic pattern that can turn ordinary list into a poem. Using words outlined in the lesson, students can create list poems of their identities.

1. Students can choose from this list of sentences stems:

   I am…
   I have…
   I can…
   I hope…
   I wish…

2. Students are encouraged to include items that highlight their personal, social, and racial identities.

3. To create the poem, students can
   • repeat stems
   • arrange statements in an order that they think works best

- repeat the first line of at the beginning and conclusion of the poem; e.g., *My name is… ,*

Lesson: Who Am I? Who Are You?

This activity encourages students to think about their personal, social, and racial identities and to compare them to those in their classroom community.

1. Using the Who Am I? reproducible on page 94, students fill in a number of items related to identity. Some students might be unsure about how to answer or may, in fact, choose to leave an item blank.
2. Students work in pairs to create a Venn diagram. Each circle is labelled with a partner's name. Where the Venn areas intersect, partners list things that they have in common.
3. Students meet in groups of four to compare Venn diagrams. As a group, students can list things that all four people have in common.
4. As a class, discuss:
   - Was it easy/comfortable for you to fill in each circle?
   - What are some items you included in the empty circles?
   - Which of these items are personal identities? Which are social identities?
   - How did this activity help you to think about embracing diversity?

PERSPECTIVE

A Sense of Belonging

by Cheryll Duquette

Cheryll Duquette's book *Finding a Place for Every Student* offers effective strategies for creating inclusive classrooms where all students belong and can learn. Duquette presents a comprehensive guide to help teachers meet the challenges they face today to include students with different strengths, needs, learning styles, interests, and cultural backgrounds.

Student belonging at school is not a given. It takes a teacher who is willing to work towards developing positive and trusting relationships with their students, supporting academic success, and encouraging peer acceptance to ensure that every student feels as though they have a place in the classroom

Belonging is one of psychologist Maslow's (1970) basic human needs. It involves the feelings of being connected, and of being accepted, respected, included, and supported by others. The student–teacher relationship is the foundation of a student's sense of belonging. As teachers, we need to establish a relationship based on trust and respect, and to ensure, through words and actions, that each student is accepted by peers and that every student experiences academic success. Research has shown that a sense of belonging is related to motivation and academic achievement. Many students have trouble working and learning unless they feel the teacher likes them and is genuinely trying to help them succeed. Moreover, students need to be able to expect that their peers will not bully or harass them; rather, that they will collaborate with them in group work and accept them outside the classroom walls.

Some students will require explicit instruction to practice and develop basic social skills. The basic social skills outlined here should be developed so that a student is accepted by peers:

- Working collaboratively with peers
- Disagreeing appropriately and receiving criticism
- Respecting others' points of view
- Conflict resolution and social problem-solving
- Regulating emotions and behavior
- Treating everyone with respect and kindness

See *Dramathemes, 4th edition* by Larry Swartz for further suggestions for drama games that focus on communication, creativity, personal narratives, fostering inclusion, and embracing diversity.

Since certain issues might be sensitive for some participants, students can be given a choice of standing/stepping forward or not.

Lesson: Who's in the Room?

Each of us is the same and yet different; the differences can cause exclusion, distrust, and fear. Participating in a cooperative game or drama activity provides students with opportunities to consider the idea of acceptance and focus on embracing diversity.

1. Students can sit at their desks or stand. Ideally, students sit in chairs in a circle so that they can see one another as the activity unfolds.
2. Call out different criteria. Some examples:

   Stand if…
   - Your birthdate is an odd number
   - You had a sandwich for lunch
   - You took the bus to school
   - You have a younger brother
   - You have won a prize
   - You own a cat
   - You have been on a camping trip
   - You have read all the Percy Jackson novels

3. If the criterion applies to them, players acknowledge by raising a hand or standing and shouting, "That's me!" An alternative approach is to have students stand in a circle and step forward if an item applies to them. As they show identification with the criterion, students are encouraged to notice others they might have something in common with.
4. As students become more familiar with the game, you might choose to add topics that would reveal details connected to their culture and identity; for example,

   Stand if…
   - You were born in this country
   - You can speak more than two languages
   - You attend or have attended a school particular to your heritage
   - At least one of your grandparents immigrated to this country
   - You know the story of how you were named
   - You know someone who uses the pronouns *they/them*

Extension

As a follow-up to this activity students can
- Share stories about one of the announced items
- Notice and share connections they have to others in the class
- Discuss how they felt about playing this game. What can we learn by playing this game?

Lesson: What's Your Name?

Versions this activity have appeared in previous publications by Larry Swartz: *Deepening In-Class and Online Learning; Take Me to Your Readers; Write to Read.*

Everyone has a name. Everyone's name is different from that of the person beside them. Everyone has a story about their name. Listening to everyone's story helps students recognize and accept the diversity of those they work and learn with from day to day. When we invite students think about their names, we are inviting them to think about how we got our names, the significance of names, the meaning behind our names, and sometimes the challenges of spelling or pronouncing our names. Recalling personal narratives about names, sharing them orally with others, and writing these stories help us all connect to our identities and cultures, and to each other.

These picture books are ideal anchor texts for name narratives:

Alma and How She Got Her Name by Juana Martinez-Neal
My Name is Yoon by Helen Recorvits; illus. Gabi Swiatkowska
The Name Jar by Yangsook Choi
Thao by Thao Lam
Your Name is a Song by Jamilah Thompkins-Bigelow; illus. Luisa Uribe

1. To begin, tell students a story about your first and last name. Ask: *What information did you learn from the story? What questions might you ask to learn more about the name?*
2. Provide students with list of questions to help them think about their names.

   - Why did your parents choose to give you this name?
   - Were you named after someone?
   - Do you have nickname? How did you get it?
   - Do you like your name?
   - Do you know your name in other languages?
   - If you could choose another name, what might it be? Why?
   - What, if anything, is unique about the spelling of your first name? Of your last name?
   - Do you know the meaning of your name?
   - Do you know any family members, celebrities, historical figures, authors, or fictional characters who share your first name with you?

3. To prepare for oral and written narratives, students answer as many questions as will help them reflect on different aspects of their first, middle, and/or last name.
4. Students meet in groups of five or six. Each student should have a chance to tell a story about their name. The answers to the questions can be used to guide the storytelling.
5. The whole class meets, perhaps sitting in a circle to enrich community storytelling. Each student is given up to one minute to tell the whole-class group a story about their name.
6. After sharing stories out loud, have students write personal narratives using information they shared with others.
7. Some students might reveal how their names have caused them some stress. Students could have nicknames that they like, but may share stories how people have made fun of their first and last name. Discuss: Why would someone tease others about their names? How is making fun of someone's name a hateful activity?

My name is Mia and I love it! My parents were going to name me Summer because I was born on summer solstice. I'm glad they named me Mia.

My mom and dad named me Jeremy. They told me that when I was born, they each decided to make a list of three names they liked. They both had the name Jeremy on it.

My name is Georgia. In Latin it means "farmer's daughter." My parents chose the name because my dad LOVES music (me too!). When my mom was thinking of a name for a girl, she thought of Georgia, and of course my dad loved it because of the jazzy song "Georgia on My Mind."

My name is sometimes a problem for me because some people make fun of it. Even though I try get to used to it, I ask: Why would someone tease me about the name I was born with? To tell you the truth, I love my name but hate when someone makes fun of it. Do they know how I feel? Do they hate me?

Yes, I have a long, long name. I always get worried when a teacher or substitute tries to pronounce it. I'm proud of my name and am sorry it causes people some trouble. I don't mind correcting people if they can't say my name.

Once upon a time there was a kid blessed by God, and so was born Adam.

Reflection

Students can discuss in small groups or as a whole class.

- What are some commonalities in the stories we heard?
- What are some surprises we encountered in our shared stories?
- What do name stories tell us about equity and diversity?

Extensions

1. Digital Storytelling

Each student in the class can contribute to a class digital presentation. Each member, in turn, records a short story about their name. Each student is not required to tell everything about their name, but can choose two or three essential statements that serve to tell others about the significance of their name.

2. Name Interviews

Students can interview family members, neighbors, or other members of the school community to investigate stories about their names. Stories can be written as a narrative or presented in interview format.

Lesson: I Wish You Knew...

In the nonfiction book *I Wish You Knew* by Jackie Azúa Kramer, illustrated by Magdalena Mora, a young girl's family faces trouble when her undocumented father has to return to his native country. Estrella brings her worries to school and would like her teacher to know what his going on in her life: "I wish you knew that since my father left, my mother works a lot. And my brother has bad dreams. I wish everyone knew how much I miss him." The teacher in this story also wishes that her students knew what she is thinking and feeling: "I wish they knew that when they forget their homework or sit alone at lunch, or cry over little things, they are not alone."

Often, we don't know about the lived lives and the wishes of our students. In a safe, caring environment, students can be given opportunities to *choose* to reveal some inner secrets they wish the teacher and classmates might know about them. I Wish You Knew... can help build community, compassion, and connections, as students share information, stories, and feelings about their lives. It is an activity that requires honesty, builds trust, and fosters tolerance of those who lead lives different from our own—another step in confronting hate caused by differences.

1. Distribute sticky notes to class members. Tell students that it doesn't matter how many they take (suggested maximum: 6 notes).

2. Once the notes have been distributed, tell students that they are to write down one fact about themselves on each note they have; i.e., if a player has only one sticky note, they record only one fact.
3. Emphasize to students that the facts they write can be *voluntarily* shared with others.
4. Students can work in small groups or with the whole class to inform others about something they think others might not know about themselves (but wish they did).

Reflection

- Was it easy for you to think of ideas to record on sticky notes?
- Were there any surprises you learned about others?
- What things did you find you might have in common with someone in your class?
- Without revealing secrets, were there things about yourself that you didn't feel comfortable sharing? Why not?

One day, teacher Kyle Schwartz asked her Grade 3 students to fill in the blank in this sentence: *I WISH MY TEACHER KNEW_____*. Some of the results were humorous, some heartbreaking. Many answers were moving, all were enlightening.

> I wish my teacher knew…
> *I have a scar on my leg.*
> *I sometimes cry when I watch movies.*
> *I have two mothers.*
> *I'm hungry a lot.*
> *I sleep with a stuffed animal.*
> *I go to church every week.*
> *I hate to go swimming.*

The student answers opened Schwartz's eyes to the need for educators to understand the unique realities their students face in order to create an open, safe, and supporting classroom environment. When the author shared her experience online, teachers around the globe began sharing their own contributions to #IWishMyTeacherKnew. The book *IWishMyTeacherKnew: How one question can change everything for our kids* by Kyle Schwartz provides a look at systemic problems that affect students nationwide (e.g., poverty, mobility, trauma, relationships). Kyle Schwartz's experience as an educator provides her with significant insights and research into how we can reach and teach every student. For Schwartz, reading these stories from the classroom can help educators, family members, and students consider how we can help students tackle challenges and how we can have our schools be places where we "can produce resilient, creative and passionate learners who will improve our world" (p. 219).

Unpack Stories of Hate

According to Robert Fulford, there is no such thing as *just* a story. Fulford emphasizes that a story is always charged with meaning, otherwise it is not a story, merely a sequence of events. When we provide activities for students to reflect upon stories that have happened to them or stories they may have witnessed, that they have heard about, or perhaps that they have invented in a dramatic context, we are providing students with a space to make sense of—to give meaning to—their stories. Because we are human, we have a multitude of narratives swimming inside of us. For Harold Rosen (1988), "narrative is nothing if not a supreme means of re-ordering otherwise chaotic, shapeless events into a coherent whole, saturated with meaning" (p. 164).

Story enables students to give shape to their life experiences through recounting them, perhaps comparing them with literary, real, or personal stories of others. Personal narrative is a powerful way of validating one's own life to oneself and to others. What may, at first, be fleeting memories gain significance when they are told out loud, in pairs, small groups, or the whole class. When students tell stories, they bring others into their worlds. Moreover, students can hitchhike on one another's ideas to tell stories from their own lives.

In this section, students are given opportunities to reveal their life experiences, to help them build a dimension of who they are, what they are thinking and feeling. When digging into issues connected to hate and discrimination, the world of story probably best helps students think about events that have led to hateful words or actions and consider how these events were dealt with (or not). Stories told, stories read, stories written, stories dramatized, fictional stories, stories from the media, and, most significantly, personal stories help bring authenticity to the topic of hate and microaggressions. Stories beget stories, and in this chapter we offer lessons—and real stories from real students—that can help students narrate, ask questions, think about what they would do and should do when encountering hate, and consider what the story means in order to prevent, confront, and disrupt hate.

Lesson: The Crumple Person

Hateful behavior often presents itself as name-calling or slurs about someone's race, religion, gender, abilities, class, or culture. This lesson challenges students to consider the issue of name-calling and put-downs.

For this activity, a large cut-out shape of a human body is needed. One student can volunteer to lie down in a neutral position (arms and legs should be outstretched) on a large sheet of paper while a partner traces the outline of the body. The outline is then cut out.

Part A: Creating a Crumple Person

1. Have students sit in a circle. Introduce the cut-out human form to the group with a gender-neutral name (e.g., Chris, Jess, Pat).
2. Inform students that "Jess" is not doing well today at school. Jess has been harassed and bullied over the past week. Jess has been called a number of hateful names that have been hurtful.
3. Students consider what put-down names Jess might have heard at school.
4. Invite students to volunteer to record a put-down term that Jess might have heard. Students, in turn, are given a marker to write the term somewhere on

"Each time a child describes an experience he or someone else has had, he constructs part of his past, adding to his sense of who he is and conveying it to others." — Susan Engel, author of *The Stories Children Tell* (1995, p. 1)

With thanks to Vanessa Russell

Some put-downs can be considered sensitive because of their sexual, racial, or cultural intent. This activity encourages students to be trusting of each other; they are invited to volunteer these slurs to help them consider the meaning and intent of the terms. Although this is a powerful activity, sensitivity is required on the part of teacher and students for all to participate appropriately.

the cut-out body. With each derogatory name, the figure is crumpled once by the student who identified the put-down word.

5. The activity continues, with volunteers coming forward. Some may choose to record more than one item. Some may choose to remain silent during the activity. Provide wait time, if necessary, for students to come forward.

6. As a final activity with markers, Jess can be displayed up-close to each student sitting in the circle. Students can choose to add a name or not.

Part B: Uncrumpling

1. Once the figure is entirely crumpled, ask students: *How is Jess different from before? How do you think Jess feels? How do you think Jess might act or behave?*

2. Ask students to consider how they might be able to help Jess feel better. What could people at Jess's school say or do to help Jess? With each suggestion, invite a student to come forward and smooth over a place where Jess has been "harmed." It is not necessary for student to uncrumple their own derogatory comment.

3. The activity continues until Jess has been entirely uncrumpled.

Part C: Reflecting on Hateful Put-downs

1. Ask students: *How is Jess different from the beginning of the class? How might Jess feel now? What might Jess's future be like?* Discuss how Jess's "scars" or creases show how put-downs might have a lasting effect.

2. As a class, discuss how we can ensure that no one gets crumpled in the class or school community. What are some ground rules and group norms that need to be considered? Are these realistic? Can there be consequences if the rules are broken?

3. Students record their feelings about the activity: How did they feel throughout? How did the activity help them to think of hateful, bullying behavior? How did this activity connect to their own experiences or to those of someone they know?

Extensions

Although the activity can be considered most powerful when shared with a group sitting in a circle, some teachers have presented similar activities as follows:

- Students work in pairs or small groups to write put-downs on a character figure. This character might be connected to a bullied or tormented character in a novel they have read.
- In lieu of crumpling, make tears in the cut-out figure. The wounds can then be taped together.
- The activity can be done using nails hammered on a board. Each time a put-down is offered, students hammer a nail into a block of wood. The nails can be removed, with the holes left as scars.

Lesson: Stories of Hate

The stories of our lives are swimming in our heads. When we talk with others, these stories often pop out of our mouths, released by the human need to share them with others. When we are at social gatherings, at family celebrations, in the hallways at school, eating a meal, shopping, playing, we tell stories about what has happened to us, to people we know, or to people we've heard or read about. Sometimes a book, movie, play, or news report is a reminder of things that have happened to us. Often, when others tell stories, our own are awakened, and when we are comfortable with people, we choose to reveal the stories that swim in our heads.

Alas, students of all ages have experienced or witnessed stories of being teased or taunted, perhaps being bullied or harassed. In a safe, caring classroom, students' stories can be shared with classmates, fostering human connection and compassion. Moreover, listening to personal stories helps brings authenticity to the issue of hate and provides contexts for discussing such things as "What did you do?" "What should you do?" to help prepare students for encountering such events.

Here are three ways to inspire narratives:

1. **Read aloud** a picture book, novel excerpt, poem, or news report to the class.
   Before the Story: Activate prior experience by asking a question that invites students to make connections to the content or theme
   During the Story: Encourage spontaneous responses; we cannot plan for what will trigger a memory.
   After the Story: Ask, "Was there anything in the story that reminded you of something from your own life, or the life of someone you know?"

2. **Share your own story.** When teachers share their own stories about hate, they demonstrate how they make personal connections and choose to share the story with the students as trusted audience.

3. **Provide students with a choice of topics** related to hate to consider by giving them a list:

   Do you have a story about…?
   - Racism
   - Homophobia
   - Transphobia
   - Islamophobia
   - Antisemitism
   - Ableism
   - Classism
   - Bullying

Teaching Tips

- My Story, Your Story: Remind students that the story need not have happened to them personally. They may have a story about hate that happened to a friend, that happened to a family member, that they know from media or social media.

- Talk Before Writing: Oral narrative prepares students to preserve their stories in writing, giving significance to their personal narrative. When students share stories out loud, they are rehearsing their thoughts in writing. Students can share stories in pairs or in small groups before sharing with the whole class.

- Choosing to Share: Some students may feel a) that they don't have a story to contribute to the discussion or b) embarrassed or ashamed, and not comfortable about sharing their stories. Talk involves listening *and* speaking; encourage students to listen to the stories of others. When students listen to the courage others have in sharing their stories, they may choose to share their own stories. Also, some stories told by their friends might prompt stories from their own lives.

- Writing is Personal: Students can share their written stories in small groups. Some might feel comfortable sharing them with the whole class. Some students may choose to keep these stories private. Written stories provide an opportunity for students to recount a story from their lives. When ready,

These lessons deal with some very sensitive issues, experiences, and language that might pose a trigger risk in the classroom. It is recommended that teachers use their knowledge of and relationship with their students to ensure that only lessons in which everyone can participate appropriately and safely are used.

students can share these stories outside the lesson with a trusted friend, teacher, or family member.

After being presented with the question *What is Hate?*, middle-grade students in one school were invited to share personal narratives. Teachers provided students with a list of topics to consider and time was given for students to share their stories in groups of two or three. As a final activity, students were instructed to write a story inspired by the out-loud stories shared in discussions. Here are some examples of students' responses to the question *Do you have a story about hate?*

When I was in Grade 3, I was made fun of because of the food I ate. One of the things had coconut in it and this kid asked me, "Is that bird poop?" For a long time after that I didn't eat that food but now I learned to love my food and my culture. My culture matters. If I saw that kid today I would probably eat my food in front of him without thinking twice. Maybe I'd offer him some. — S. P., Grade 7

Very recently, someone came up to my friend and tugged on both our hijabs. We shouted that that wasn't okay but this person just shrugged and walked off. This action infuriated us and made us feel uncomfortable. — M.S., Grade 8

I used to have a friend that was always teased because of her name. Why would someone be hateful to someone just because of their name? — T.J., Grade 6

This is a story told in my family. My grandparents went on a holiday in the United States. They went into a store and my Grandma asked the clerk "Is there a bathroom I can use?" and the clerk said "There are no bathrooms for 'N-word." My grandparents walked out. The lesson learned is there will always be racism. — N.V., Grade 7

A girl with a hijab
"Take it off" they said.
"You're a terrorist!" they said.
"Go back to your country!" they said.
The girl stayed strong.
And proudly wears her hijab.
— S.A., Grade 8

I think I was 10 when this happened. I was walking with my friend and a white kid came put to us and called us slaves and "the N-word." At that time, I didn't even know what "the N-word" meant. But that guy must have hated us just because our skin was different from his. So sad. — N.K., Grade 7

A racist person appeared on one of the social media I go to and spammed extremely racist words until he got banned. However, he started a new account and kept spamming and each time he got banned. He starts a new account every time until his IP gets banned. Moral: Beware racism on social media. — A.S., Grade 6

This happened last year to my mother who was riding a public transit bus. A man filled with hatred was yelling and screaming. I was at home awaiting my mother's arrival. Now, my mother is a very strong and independent person. It's rare to see her tear up but when she opened our front door, I heard her sniffling and I knew something was wrong. I never learned what the man was shouting but it is so upsetting to know that people hate each other. My mother told me that nobody on the bus, even the driver, did anything to stop the man. — W.H., Grade 8

This story takes place in a group chat where there are many people. It all started when me and my friends were talking about school and one guy "Josh" said a gay slur at me. My friend started telling this person off but Josh kept repeating and repeating the word. We tried to tell him it was wrong but one thing led to another and it turned to really bad insults. "You are a terrorist. Go bomb a building!" Nothing got resolved that day except we kicked him out of groupchat. It's one thing to have thick skin but I think we need to stop talking to people when they say hurtful things.
— F.K., Grade 8

Recently my Pakistani friend had henna on her hand which is a tradition in our culture, but someone told her that it looked disgusting which offended both of us. — M.F., Grade 8

Two weeks ago some older kids made fun of my friend because he is short. My friend didn't really care but if that happened to other people, they could get upset. Why can't people learn not to make fun of other people because of their physical challenges? — W.H., Grade 6

My dad and I were watching television and there were some really bad stories about antisemitism. I think hate is bad and I would like to end it. I don't really know any Jewish people but if there was a swastika displayed in my school I would try to do something about it. Wouldn't you?
— A.J., Grade 8

Lesson: Exploring Images of Hate

When students Google "images of hate," they will find thousands of visuals, including illustrations and photographs. Every picture tells a story, so for this activity, invite students to inspect and reflect on visuals that foster narrative, evoke feelings, and raise questions. Most of the pictures on the Google Images site are drawn from real-life incidents. As students investigate and respond to the faces, the words, and the scenarios presented here, they can better make connections to what hate looks like and feels like.

Digging Deep into an Image

Invite students to choose at least one image of hate from Google Images. Have students complete the following statements:

1. I chose this image because…
2. A title I would give to accompany this image is…
3. I think this picture tells the story of…
4. When I look at this image, I feel…
5. When I look at this image, I wonder… (at least two statements)

Students meet in groups of four or five to discuss their responses to the images. How were the images similar or different?

Extension: Students can create an illustration to represent a moment in time before the picture they have chosen OR a moment in time following the picture they have chosen (or perhaps two images, one before and one after).

Images for a Book Cover

1. Invite students to investigate a range of images and decide upon one or two that they would choose to include as the cover of a book entitled *Stop the Hate*.
2. Students work in groups of five or six to share their choices and share their findings. Each student can be given the opportunity to persuade others why their choice should be used by a publisher.
3. As an editorial committee, students can choose one image they think captures the theme of stopping hate. Then each group presents its choice to the whole class.

Extension: Students can design a *Stop the Hate* book cover using the image of choice. They should consider the following: How will the picture be displayed? How much space will the title have? What font and color will be used in their book cover design?

Media Reports

Many photographs that appear in Google Images are directly related to world-wide events of hate incidents. Students can use an image of choice to research and prepare a report about hate and discrimination. Tell the students to imagine that the photograph they have chosen appeared on the front page of a newspaper or magazine. Students can then write a report answering the questions *Who?*, *What?*, *Where?*, *When?*, and *Why?* that would appear on the front page to accompany this visual. What headline might be used to draw readers attention to the story?

Here are some samples of images of hate in media reports

- From: https://www.voanews.com/a/usa_two-men-seattle-san-francisco-face-anti-asian-hate-charges/6203849.html
The image shows the collection of anti-Asian and Black hate. The Chinese slogan means "Defeating White Supremacy".
- From https://www.syracuse.com/opinion/2022/11/political-rhetoric-emboldens-perpetrators-of-hate-against-lgbtq-community-your-letters.html
- From: https://religionnews.com/2020/07/15/will-the-death-of-george-floyd-sway-white-evangelicals-on-race/
Recreating the scene of George Floyd being restrained
- From: https://www.nbcnews.com/nbc-out/out-news/anti-gay-hate-crimes-fell-slightly-2020-anti-trans-crimes-rose-fbi-say-rcna1846
In NYC, Brooklyn "Black Trans Lives Matter"
- From: https://theconversation.com/how-canada-committed-genocide-against-indigenous-peoples-explained-by-the-lawyer-central-to-the-determination-162582
A silent protest against Residential Schools
- From: https://rafu.com/2022/01/subway-killing-shocks-asian-americans-coast-to-coast/
- From: https://www.bbc.com/news/world-us-canada-54968498
- From: https://www.pbs.org/newshour/nation/2021-is-now-the-deadliest-year-on-record-for-transgender-people

Personal Story

Last week in our school, a Jewish boy discovered a Swastika symbol painted on the door of his locker. Why would someone do that? Many people in my class knew that this symbol was connected to Hitler but I think some people in my class didn't even know how this hate graffiti would be so offensive to Jewish people today. — Max O., Grade 7

PERSPECTIVE

The Swastika as an Image of Hate

by Larry Swartz

For Jewish people, the swastika is seen as a symbol of wanting to destroy Jewish people, particularly since it triggers the horrors of the Holocaust. It is frightening to know that, in our world, the swastika is drawn in schools, in religious centres, and on community walls daily.

Students may be aware of the swastika as a symbol of hate, but might not be aware of its history and its significance to Antisemitism. To avoid misunderstanding and misuse, it is important to provide students with information about the swastika and provide them with an opportunity to raise questions about its significance with the issues of hate of discrimination. The following questions, discussed in small groups or as a whole class, can help build understanding of how labels and symbols can contribute to the rise of such ideologies as white supremacy…

- What is the history of the swastika?
- Why is the swastika considered to be the strongest symbol of those who hate?
- How is the swastika used today? How might its use be hurtful or inflammatory?
- How do you feel when you see a swastika image in the news? In movies? Spray-painted hate graffiti?
- What might you do if you see someone spray-painting a swastika on a wall?
- Besides the swastika, what are some other symbols of hate?

The United States Holocaust Memorial Museum offers some important facts about the swastika. Here are 6 key facts that can be shared with students to have them reflect on this symbol's past and present.

1. The word *swastika* comes from the Sanskrit *svastika*, which means "good-fortune" or "well-being."
2. The swastika has been used as a symbol of well-being in ancient societies (e.g., China, India, Africa). The earliest known swastika is from 10 000 BC.
3. The Nazi party formally adopted the swastika as its symbol in 1920. In Germany, the symbol is known as *Hakenkreuz*, which means "hooked cross."
4. Adolf Hitler designed the Nazi flag by combining the swastika with the colors of the German Imperial flag (red, black, and white).

5. The Nazi party was not the only party to use the swastika in Germany. A number of far-right movements adopted the swastika as a symbol of a "racially pure" state.
6. The use of propaganda and the swastika is banned and prohibited by law, even in Germany. Individuals violating such terms may be subject to criminal proceedings in most countries.

Lesson: Creating Images of Hate

This activity invites students to create illustrations to show interpretations of what hate looks like. To keep it simple, provide students with a blank piece of paper and a black marker. Instruct students to create a picture that depicts hate in some form. Students may wish to illustrate a scene that tells a story of hatred; some may wish to convey hate through abstract images. Limiting the amount of time (e.g., up to 30 minutes) allows students' drawings to be a spontaneous response that reveals what they think hate looks like using visual images.

Tips
- Students can create an illustration drawn from real-life experiences.
- Students can create art work from imagined situations.
- Adding words, perhaps through speech or thought bubbles, is optional.
- Encourage students to convey emotions through images of facial expressions or body language.

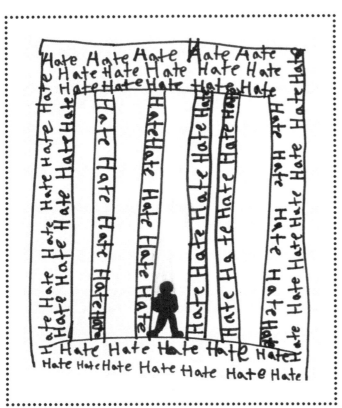

Extensions

1. Once the images of hate are completed, they can be interpreted. Students gather in a circle, each bringing their completed drawing. Students pass their illustrations clockwise around the circle, in silence. On a signal, students are instructed to examine and interpret the image that is now in their hands. Students then turn and talk to a neighbor or neighbors and share their interpretations by considering
   - Is there a story being told?
   - What emotions are being conveyed?
   - What questions come to mind about this image?
   - Does this illustration remind you of real-life events?

   Students then continue to pass the artwork around the circle until each person receives their own. Students can volunteer to share and describe their illustrations.

2. Instead of creating illustrations using only black marker on white paper, how might students show what hate looks like if using various colored markers, oil or chalk pastels, paint, construction paper, plasticine, collage, computer graphics?

Explore Literature

"When the reader stands in his own world view, unable to see or conceive of any other perspective, a book can be a bridge. The right book at the right time can span the divide between where the reader stands in this moment and alternate views, new ideas and options are considered."

— Lester L. Laminack and Katie Kelly, from *Reading To Make a Difference* (2019, xiii)

Books, especially books described as multicultural, can be the means to address the tough topic of hate that can arise in the classroom, in the schoolyard, in the community, and in students' lives. Some children's literature not only offers an alternative way of looking at the world but also gives voice to people whose perspectives are rarely heard or, if heard, are not valued. An expansion in the publishing of multicultural children's literature has meant that now there are many more titles reflecting how some groups of people have felt oppressed or discriminated against. Children' literature increasingly presents worlds that expose students to how people outside their experience live and struggle. Multicultural literature not only focuses on matters of race and ethnicity, but also addresses such topics as sexual orientation, ableism, religion, and immigration and refugee experiences. It also celebrates individuals who act to improve the lives of people subject to factors that limit what they can be and do.

Whenever we choose multicultural picture books, novels, poetry, and nonfiction titles for use in our classrooms, we must consider how well they address social justice goals, such as belonging, acceptance, and equity; how well they foster a sense of inclusion and confront intolerance and hate. In a classroom community of readers, students can meet characters, both real and fictional, who reflect or affirm their cultural identities, opening their minds to accept differences and opening their hearts to interpret differences with tolerance and kindness. Books allow readers to see themselves as global citizens—to understand their own beliefs, relationships, and values and to consider how to act on them.

Why use children's literature to build understanding of hate and discrimination? Children's literature helps

- To make **connections**: Students may choose to reveal their stories when reading a text, thus making connections between the realities, desires, intentions, and emotions of the characters and those of their own lives.
- To **resolve problems** and learn from characters who might draw from unexpected resources, conversations, and actions in ways that might not have occurred to the reader.
- To raise **questions** about topics of concern leading to **inquiry** about an issue.
- To learn about the **identities** and **cultures** of others, providing a window into their lives and perspectives and supporting a deeper and more well-rounded understanding of themselves in relation to others.
- To explore narratives that serve as **case studies** for relationships, values, and struggles; case studies that include multiple perspectives and provide useful background information about issues of social inequity, marginalization, and oppression.
- To serve as **artifacts** for meaningful response (i.e., discussion, writing, media, the arts, etc.).

For an independent reading project on Identity, Discrimination and Hate, the students in Mrs. Stein's Grade 7 class read these fictional titles.

Arsalan A./*The Good War* by Todd Strasser (racism, white supremacy)

Tal A./*Monster* by Walter Dean Myers (anti-Black racism)

AJ B./*Ghost Boys* by Jewell Parker Rhodes (anti-Black racism)

Zev D./*Drama* by Raina Telgemeier (bullying)

Yzavera D./*The Benefits of Being an Octopus* by Ann Braden (poverty, classism)

Eli D./*The Children of Willesden Lane* by Mona Golabek and Lee Cohen, adapted by Emil Sher (antisemitism; the Holocaust)

Ethan F./*It Wasn't Me* by Dana Alison Levy (identity; restorative justice)

Simon F./*The Boy in the Striped Pajamas* by John Boyne (antisemitism, the Holocaust)

Ruiya H./*The Many Meanings of Meilan* by Andrea Wang (anti-Asian racism)

David K./*The Other Boy* by M.G. Hennessey (transphobia)

Tivaun L./*A Place to Belong* by Cynthia Kadohata (anti-Asian racism)

Seth R./*Two Degrees* by Alan Gratz (climate change)

Sarah T./*Under the Iron Bridge* by Kathy Kacer (antisemetism; the Holocaust)

Arman T./*Blended* by Sharon M. Draper (racial identity)

William W./*Prairie Lotus* by Linda Sue Park (anti-Asian Racism)

Simon W./*Restart* by Gordon Korman (bullying)

Simona Y./*When Stars Are Scattered* by Omar Mohamed and Victoria Jamieson (refugee experience)

Chloe Y./*Posted* by John David Anderson (bullying, social media)

Nathan Y./*New Kid* by Jerry Craft (racial identity, classism)

Mrs. Stein/*Linked* by Gordon Korman (antisemitism)

Lesson: The Word *Hate* in Fiction

See page 21 for Lesson: Responding to Quotations for more work with quotes.

See page 95 for Fictional Words of Hate, a list of excerpts from novels. Each of the quotations from narration or dialogue in a novel contains the word *hate*. Here are three suggested options for having students respond to these statements.

Discussing Excerpts

Students meet in groups of three or four to review and discuss the excerpts that appear in the reproducible. Have each group member choose one item to respond to and then discuss:

• What does this excerpt say about hate?
• What story do you think is connected to this excerpt?
• What questions come to mind about who is making this statement?

Thinking Stem Responses

Invite students to choose one excerpt from this list and then complete the following thinking stems:

I'm reminded of…
I predict…
I wonder….

Students meet in groups of four or five to share their thinking stem responses.

Revisiting the Novel

If students are familiar with any of the novels mentioned on the list, invite them to tell others about the novel and discuss how hate might have been part of the story. If the books are available, have students choose to read one of the novels independently.

Extension: Following this activity, students might be conscious of finding the word *hate* as they continue to read a novel. Encourage students to record statements of narration or dialogue from novels that they encounter. As a class project, students can prepare a list of fictional quotations featuring the word *hate*.

Lesson: Perspective Writing

This activity involves writing in role from the perspective of a character in a familiar format such as a letter, diary, text message, or interview. Students step into another's shoes and examine the world from that point of view by retelling events in the first person. Writing from the perspective of someone who has experienced hate or discrimination, or perhaps was witness to an event, helps students develop empathy for the character and the situation. In their writing, students are encouraged to give detailed information about the incident, and discuss the relationships that the character has, as well as the feelings that the character might have.

Teaching Tip: Exploring Role-playing

1. Engaging students in initial role-playing activities such as hot-seating or interviewing can provide a motivation for the perspective-writing activity.
2. Once students have completed a perspective-writing activity, they can present it to a partner, a small group, or the whole class. Students, as fictional characters, can be interviewed by others to learn more about the story and reveal more about the discrimination problem and how it was solved.

Character Journal or Diary Entry

Invite students to write a journal or diary entry from a character's perspective. Students write in the first person to retell story events, describe what is happening, discuss a problem and how it has been solved (or not), and express emotions about a character's experiences. Character journals can recount a single event or perhaps several entries written over time.

> *Dear Diary,*
>
> *Today Mama brought me to the new school to get registered. We met the principal, Mr Reynard. I instantly felt his fake smile radiating awkwardness of being around an Asian person. He proceed to tell Mama that my name was too different and would make me stand out. Mr Reynard suggested changing my name from Meilan to Melanie and Mama agreed without even asking for my opinion. I was so frustrated and wanted to yell at Mr. Reynard that my Chinese name was perfectly fine. Of course I didn't because I knew Mama would yell at me. When we got home I started complaining to Baba but the only thing he said was méi bàn fã. Nothing to be done. Really?????*
>
> *Love*
> *Hua Meilan*

These lessons deal with some very sensitive issues, experiences, and language that might pose a trigger risk in the classroom. It is recommended that teachers use their knowledge of and relationship with their students to ensure that only lessons in which everyone can participate appropriately and safely are used.

Book Title: *The Many Meanings of Meilan* by Andrea Wang
Character Journal written by Ruiya H, Grade 7

Fictional Text Messages, Emails, or Letters

Tell students to imagine that they have the opportunity to text message a character from a story. What opinions, questions, and reactions would they have of that character's life? The exchange can continue by having the character respond by writing a fictitious email message in response. Students may wish to do this in pairs, with one person assuming the role of a character and the second person playing themselves. As an alternative, students may choose to each write two or more email messages between two characters. An alternative approach to this activity is to have students write a letter from a character. Who might they send the letter to? What might the reply be?

Hanna: Hello!

Joel: Hi Hanna. I'm Joel. How are you feeling these days?

Hanna. Not the best.

Joel. Why not?

Hanna: I just moved to a new town called LaForge Dakota. There seems to be hatred against me and my father, just because we're newcomers in this frontier town.

Joel: Yikes, that's bad. Do you have someone to talk to?

Hanna: It's hard being Asian in an allwhite town. (I'm only part Asian).

Joel: I thought my life was bad.

Hanna: What's going on with you?

Joel: I guess I'm ok… but I'm unhappy too because the way people treat me.

Hanna: Do you wanna talk about it?

Joel: I was bullied so much at my old school, mainly by this guy named Chase. I had to leave. Now I'm in a boarding school. It's really hard trying to fit in. I guess every school has bullies.

Hanna: Why do you feel that people hate you?

Joel: Everyone seems to have a great talent. I'm just not one of those musical people. I love the piano but I don't want to live and breathe it. I feel discriminated against cause 'I'm not one of them'.

Hanna: I think you and I have something in common. It's hard when others make fun of you just because of your race or your interests?

Joel: Do you think we can change the prejudices that others have against us?

Hanna: Maybe things will get better over time. It's good to have someone to talk to (even if it's just text messages)

Newspaper Article

This writing activity encourages readers to retell story events that might be reported in an article. As journalists students can answer *Who, What, Where, When, Why,* and *How* questions to report a story about discrimination or a hateful incident. A headline or illustration (to represent a newspaper photograph) might accompany the article.

June 12th, 2010

Will the world ever be safe for Black youth?

Jerome Rogers, age 12, was brutally taken out of this world. Yesterday, the innocent Black boy was shot down by a white officer who thought Jerome was carrying a gun. It was a toy gun. This is yet another story of racial profiling where police do not seem to like or trust Black people in the neighborhoods of Chicago.

Jerome's mother said that she was always fearful of her son and daughter getting through each day in their neighborhood. Through sobbing tears, Mrs. Rogers said "in this neighborhood, getting a child to adulthood is perilous. I wonder if that officer would have reacted differently if my son's skin color was white."

A toy gun. A suspicious, aggressive policeman. A dead youth who has entered heaven joining Emmett Till, Trayvon Martin and Tamir Rice and other Black Boys who can share in Jerome's story. Will things ever change? Would Jerome Rogers still be alive if he lived in a "better" neighborhood? Does living in a better neighborhood shield Black youth from racism and being targeted police? Do Black lives matter?

Thorough investigations into the incident will be looked into over the next few days. Will Officer Moore be deemed innocent as a young dead Ghost Boy looks down from Heaven?

Persuasive Letters

Tell students to imagine that the central character in a story is being considered for an award honoring them for making a difference by effectively dealing with hate. Students can prepare a persuasive letter to convince judges that this person is worthy of an award for their exemplary qualities.

Dear Judges,

I would like to nominate Lisa Jura as a heroic individual who is worthy of recognition for an award for bravery, courage and combatting hate and discrimination.

In order to save her from Nazi persecution, Lisa's parents had to send her out of Vienna to London. Lisa was one of many children in an organized rescue effort known as Kindertransport that relocated thousands of Jewish children to the United Kingdom. In London, Lisa was surrounded by people who supported her and helped her get through the trauma of being separated from family. Lisa was passionate about playing the piano and music and consistent practice was what she held onto throughout war time. It was music that inspired her, and other displaced children in Willesden Lane.

In 1894, Alfred Dreyfus was a prisoner of the French military who was falsely accused of treason. Dreyfus wrote: "My only crime was to have been born a Jew." Lisa's only crime was that she was born Jewish and was forced, like many children, to be separated from their families who were killed in a concentration camps during World War II. This brave girl stands as a special example for all those children who survived the Holocaust and lived life with courage and hope. For these reasons, I believe, Lisa Jura is worthy of an award of honor for her strong spirit in hard times.

Yours truly
Eli D.

Interview

In the question-and-answer format, students present a written interview between a media reporter and a character from a book. To prepare for this writing activity, students can work in role to conduct an oral interview between two people.

Book Title: *A Place to Belong* by Cynthia Kadohata Interview written by Tivaun L, Grade 7

Interviewer: I am preparing an article on immigration. I am pleased to have the opportunity to speak to young people about their experiences. I'm honored to introduce readers to 12 year old Hanako Tachibana.

Hanako: Thank you for giving me the chance to tell my story.

Interviewer: Do you know why I've invited you to be interviewed?

Hanako: I think you'd like me to talk about what's happening to my family right now.

Interviewer: Are you OK talking about it?

Hanako: Well World War II just ended and even though I was born and raised in America, a lot of people hate me just because I have Japanese roots. Our family was forced to go back to Japan and abandon a life that we were used to.

Interviewer: How does that make you feel?

Hanako: Truthfully – I'm really scared.

Interviewer: Why is that?

Hanako: Mostly because all my life disappeared in the blink of an eye. My father who always seemed brave and fearless now has no hope. He makes it seem that we haven't got a good future and all that we can do is hope to survive in this new mystery land named Japan. My brother is too young to understand why we are being treated like this. I feel all alone in this world of prejudice and hate. Will I ever find a place to belong?

Lesson: Ten-Sentence Book Report

When an independent reading program is established, students are given the opportunity to choose the material they read; thus their individual needs and interests are accommodated. It is best to provide a consistent time each day for students to read independently, which can be extended into reading time outside the classroom for leisure reading done at the student's own pace. Students should be given opportunities to focus on a central issue or theme, such as hate and discrimination, and to share what the novel has meant to them through response activities that include writing, talk, media, and the arts.

The Ten-Sentence Book Report template on page 96 provides a format for students to reflect on their reading and then meet in groups to discuss the novel and share their opinions. Some students may wish to write two or three sentences for some items, but the minimum is ten sentences altogether.

Extension: A class database where students submit their reports and make recommendations for reading about hate can be established

Title of Novel: *When Stars Are Scattered*
Authors: *Omar Mohamed, Victoria Jamieson*
Number of Pages: 257   Date of Publication: 2020

Sentence 1: A summary of the novel
Omar is a boy who had to flee his home country, Somalia, with his brother Hassan, because there was a war raging on. He is supposed to live in a refugee camp temporarily, but days drag into years, he lives there for a much longer period of time.

Sentence 2: Something to know about the main character
Omar hates what life has dealt him and wants to leave the refugee camp because he feels like his future is tarnished forever. He is very protective of his younger brother.

Sentence 3: A hate problem evident in the story
Life is hard as a refugee camper because food is scarce, and so is clothing and housing. It is very hot and Omar has a difficult time caring for his brother and going to school while facing the harsh realities life throws at him.

Sentence 4: Hate/discrimination is evident in the novel in this way
Big Ali doesn't like Omar and bullies and makes fun of him. Omar has a sense of doubt when going to school for the first time, and Big Ali did everything he could to make Omar feel like he made the wrong decision.

Sentence 5: Something from the novel that reminded me of my own life (or someone I know)
Like Omar, sometimes I often feel caught between making choices in my life.

Sentence 6: A sentence from the novel that I found interesting
"But when God gives you a gift, you have to use it, right?"

Sentence 7: A question or questions about hate that I thought about as I read the novel
Did Omar find his parents? Will Hassan ever learn how to talk, other than the word 'Hooyo'? Will people make fun of Hooyoo because of he doesn't speak clearly? Will these two brothers feel that they fit in with North American society?

Sentence 8: A question or questions about hate that I thought about as I finished the novel
How happy will life be for Omar when he lives in America? Will he be discriminated against for being a refugee?

Sentence 9: Here's what I would tell someone about this novel.
It is a great book that entices the reader to learn about being a refugee in a refugee camp in Kenya. I truly felt how much hardship Omar must have gone through, and all his thought process thinking about what he would do with his life and how he would ever find a place to belong.

Sentence 10: I would rate this novel as a _9_ out of 10 because…
This book effectively captures the hardships that are faced by refugees. The book is unique because it is biographical and told in graphic format.

Recommended Literature

A Comprehensive Guide of ACC (African Caribbean and Canadian Books in Colour) provides recommended fiction and nonfiction resources for K–12 schools presented by SCFA (Sickle Cell Foundation of Alberta and EPLca (Edmonton Public Library) at 2022-02-09-ACC-Books-in-Colour.pdf

Ableism / Physical Challenges

The Crazy Man by Pamela Porter
El Deafo by Cece Bell
Fly by Alison Hughes
Insignificant Events in the Life of a Cactus by Dusti Bowling (Sequel: *Momentous Events the Life of a Cactus*)
Out of My Mind by Sharon M. Draper (Sequel: *Out of My Heart)*
Wonder by R. J. Palacio

Anti-Black Racism

Clean Getaway by Nic Stone
Freewater by Amina Luqman-Dawson
Ghost Boys by Jewell Parker Rhodes
The Hate U Give by Angie Thomas (Prequel: *Concrete Rose*) (YA)
Look Both Ways: a tale told in 10 blocks by Jason Reynolds
New Kid by Jerry Craft (graphic text) (Sequels: *Class Act; School Trip*)

Anti-Asian Racism

The Front Desk (series) by Kelly Yang
Maizy Chen's Last Chance by Lisa Yee
The Many Meanings of Meilan by Andrea Wang
A Place to Belong by Cynthia Kadohata
Prairie Lotus by Linda Sue Park
When You Trap a Tiger by Tae Keller

Anti-Indigenous Racism

The Barren Grounds by David A. Robertson (The Misewa Saga) (also *The Great Bear; The Stone Child*)
The Case of the Missing Auntie by Michael Hutchinson
Borders by Thomas King; illus. Natasha Donovan (graphic text)
Fatty Legs by Christy Jordan-Fenton & Margaret-Olemaun Pokiak-Fenton; illus. Liz Amini-Holmes (biography) (Sequel: *A Stranger at Home*)
Red Wolf by Jennifer Dance
The Secret Path by Gord Downie; illus. Jeff Lemire (graphic novel)

Antisemitism

The Good Fight by Ted Staunton; illus. Josh Rosen (graphic text)
The Good War by Todd Strasser (YA)
How To Find What You're Not Not Looking For by Veera Hiranandani
Linked by Gordon Korman
Under the Iron Bridge by Kathy Kacer (also *Broken Strings* with Eric Walters)
What We're Scared Of by Keren David

Homophobia

Answers in the Pages by David Levithan
A High Five for Glenn Burke by Phil Bildner
Felix Ever After by Kacen Callender (also *King and the Dragonflies*)
On the Line by Paul Coccia and Eric Walters

The Pants Project by Cat Clarke
Rick by Alex Gino (also *Melissa; Alice Austen Lived Here*)

Islamophobia
Count Me In by Varsha Bajaj (Islamophobia)
Everything Sad Is Untrue (a true story) by Daniel Nayeri (YA)
Flying Over Water by Shannon Hitchcock and N.H. Senzai
Other Words for Home by Jasmine Warga
Wishtree by Katherine Applegate
Yusuf Azeem is Not a Hero by Saadia Faruqi

Who Am I?

For this activity, each circle is labelled with an item connected to your identity. Complete each circle by writing an answer that applies to who you are. If you are unsure about an item, leave it blank. Five circles have no labels and you are invited to fill in any descriptions of your identity you wish to add. Once completed, you will be sharing and comparing your identity lists with others in your class.

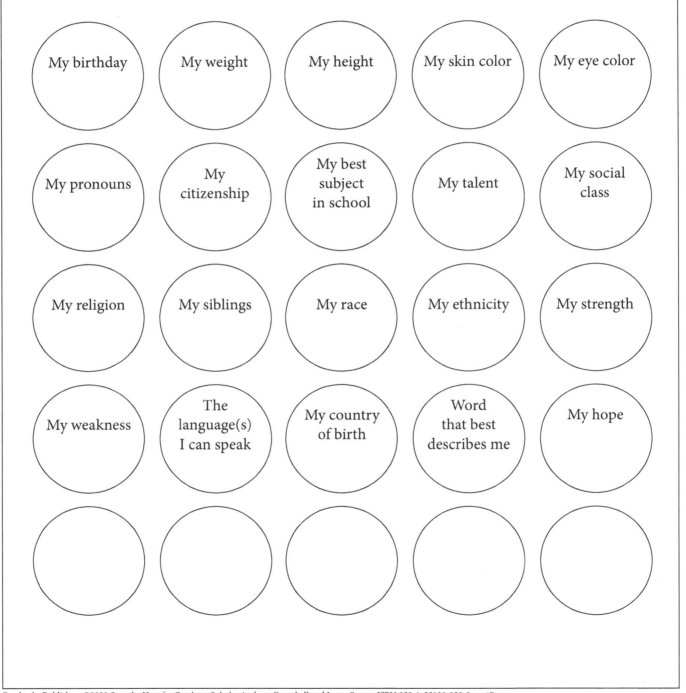

My birthday | My weight | My height | My skin color | My eye color

My pronouns | My citizenship | My best subject in school | My talent | My social class

My religion | My siblings | My race | My ethnicity | My strength

My weakness | The language(s) I can speak | My country of birth | Word that best describes me | My hope

Fictional Words of Hate

You might recognize some of these authors who talk about caring, belonging, and confronting hate, often through the characters in their novels. The word *hate* often escapes from the mouths of fictional characters. Will you find the word *hate* in the next novel you read?

Hate hurts the hater more'n the hated.
— Madeline L'Engle (*A Wrinkle in Time*)

I can **hate** you more, but I'll never love you less.
— Michael Morpurgo (*War Horse*)

Caroline was always moody and miserable, but I liked it. I liked feeling as if she had chosen me as the only person in the world not to **hate**, and so we spent all this time together just ragging on everyone, you know?
— John Green (*The Fault in the Stars*)

"If you start by **hating** one or two people, you won't be able to stop. Pretty soon you'll hate a hundred people."
"A zillion?"
"Even a zillion. **Hatred** goes a long long way. It grows and grows. And it's hungry."
— Jerry Spinelli (*Love, Stargirl*)

Nico's anger turned as cold and dark as his blade. He'd been morphed into a few plants himself and he didn't appreciate it. He **hated** people like Bryce Lawrence, who inflicted pain just for fun.
— Rick Riordan (*The Blood of Olympus*)

I'm running on **hate**.
— Suzanne Collins (*Mockingjay*)

That's the **hate** they're giving us, baby, a system designed against us. That's Thug Life.
— Angie Thomas (*The Hate U Give*)

I'd rather have anybody's **hate** than their pity.
— S.E. Hinton (*The Outsiders*)

I **hate** it when you lie. I **hate** it when you make me laugh, even worse when you make me cry. I **hate** it when you're not around, and the fact that you don't call. But mostly, I **hate** the way I don't **hate** you. Not even close, not even a little bit, not even at all.
— David Levithan (*Ten Things I Hate About You*)

The people who **hate** us can't see through the wall.
— Deborah Ellis (*My Name is Parvana*)

The word I **hate** most in the English language has to be *appropriate*.
— Gordon Korman (*The Fort*)

There's **hate** and then there's *hate*.
— Wendy Wan-Long Shang (*The Secret Battle of Evan Pao*)

"I **hate** her," Jess said through his sobs. "I **hate** her. I wish I'd never seen her in my whole life.
— Katherine Paterson (*Bridge to Terabithia*)

Sometimes I feel like he **hates** me. It's a very strange feeling. I'm not used to being **hated**.
— David Levithan (*Boy Meets Boy*)

He couldn't see that Mars Bar disliked him, maybe even **hated** him.
— Jerry Spinelli (*Maniac Magee*)

Pembroke Publishers ©2023 *Stop the Hate for Goodness Sake* by Andrew Campbell and Larry Swartz ISBN 958-1-55138-358-3

Ten-Sentence Book Report

In completing each of the statements on this page, you will have a chance to think about the main issues of the story. Although writing one-sentence responses will help you to focus on the essential features of the book, you may, if you wish, write two or three sentences to complete any of the items

Your Name: _____

Title of Novel: _____   Author: _____

Number of Pages: _____   Date of Publication: _____

Sentence 1: A summary of the novel

Sentence 2: Something to know about the main character

Sentence 3: A hate problem evident in the story

Sentence 4: Hate/discrimination is evident in the novel in this way:

Sentence 5: Something from the novel that reminded me of my own life (or someone I know)

Sentence 6: A sentence from the novel that I found interesting

Sentence 7: A question or questions about hate that I thought about as I read the novel

Sentence 8: A question or questions about hate that I thought about as I finished the novel

Sentence 9: Here's what I would tell someone about this novel

Sentence 10: I would rate this novel as a _____ (from 1 to 10) because…

Bonus: If this novel was made into a movie, here is an illustration of a scene I would expect to see in the movie. (You can use the back of this page for the drawing.)

Pembroke Publishers ©2023 *Stop the Hate for Goodness Sake* by Andrew Campbell and Larry Swartz ISBN 958-1-55138-358-3

5

Confronting the Issue of Bullying

"No student should be afraid of going to school for being harassed or degraded, and no parent should need to worry about such things happening to his or her child."
— Dr. Dan Olweus, *The Nature of School Bullying*

If I can stop one heart from breaking,
I shall not live in vain;
If I can ease one life the aching,
Or cool one pain,
Or help one fainting robin
Unto his nest again
I shall not live in vain.
— Emily Dickinson

Bullying is pervasive. Media are rife with reports of it. Many people find the problem inescapable. And bullying is not a new problem. Parents, schools, and governments have long wrestled with how to deal with the issue. In our society, where emerging technologies unite us in new ways, bullying is being recognized as an epidemic. Most students can identify and describe bullying behavior, but it is important to move beyond the basics and provide a safe forum in our classrooms to explore the complexity of the bullying web. As the complex issue of bullying continues to spin around the relationships of young people, we need to work towards a better understanding of it. We need to gain insight into why bullies behave the way they do and to recognize that a person engaging in bullying behavior is capable of showing positive actions. We also need to investigate strategies to prepare students for being caught in the triangle of the bully, the bullied, and the bystander.

According to researcher Debra Pepler, bullying is a relationship problem and needs relationship solutions. In our classrooms, we need to create social contexts that provide positive interactions. Students may disagree with others and may choose not to work alongside each person in the classroom, but every teacher, every parent, and every student has the right to expect and hope that classrooms are safe places for all. There is no room for hate in the safe space of a classroom. When we build a strong community and provide authentic contexts for students to communicate with one another, we are promoting meaningful programming that enriches student relationships. Ultimately this can guide students to making moral and ethical choices about the treatment of others. They can learn about respect in a community that thrives on respect. They can learn about acceptance, compassion, and empathy—principles that are central to a bully-free culture in the school and essential to being caring citizens of the world who strive to confront, disrupt, and stop bullying and hate.

Bullying and Hate

Bullying is a worldwide problem. A number of researchers (Dan Olweus, Peter K. Smith, Barbara Coloroso, Debra Pepler and Wendy Craig, Ken Rigby) provide statistics that reveal that the problem has not faded over the past two decades. Bullying has been found to occur once every 25 minutes in the classroom and once every seven minutes on the playground. Yearly reports from such organizations as the National Education Association and i-Safe America claim that one in three adolescent Canadian students report being bullied, which does not account for the myriad unreported cases of bullying experienced in schools. Especially when the bullying is motivated by prejudice and discrimination, it is no surprise that many people remain silent, through shame or fear of judgment from families, workplaces, or schools. Hate is a frightening concept to acknowledge. It can produce fear, confusion, anxiety, and discomfort. What is even more frightening, however, is choosing to ignore the hate that exists in the world and allowing it to fester. Unchallenged hatred can perpetuate itself, particularly for students who are in a position of vulnerability.

How Are Bullying and Hate Different?

Not all bullies hate their victims for being who they are. Not all victims of bullying hate the bully and what they represent. A bully might choose to taunt, tease, or harass someone because they want to have some power over them. The reasons for doing so might not be related to race, religion, disability, or sexual or gender identity. The intent of the bully is to harass, to cause fear in, or to intend to harm a target over time; their behavior can be considered hateful, but not necessarily because of prejudice or hate. Someone who is being bullied is likely to feel hurt, stressful, anxious, or worried. They would, of course, hate the verbal or physical attacks of the bully, but ethically or morally would not feel hatred towards this person just because of their identity.

Bullying Can Be Motivated by Hate

Why do bullies behave the way they do? There is no single answer to that question: a bully might feel insecure about themselves, might have been bullied themselves and take it out on others, or might think that they can get away with having control over others. They might choose targets who are vulnerable and try to gain power over them. A bully might behave the way they do because they dislike something the target has done or said. Like hate, bullying is a learned behavior. It can be disrupted. It can be changed.

Some of the time (not always), bullies pick their targets because of bias or prejudice against their race, religious belief, or sexuality. When trying to understand bullies, it can be challenging to get into their hearts and minds to determine why they choose to behave the way they do, but clearly their feelings and beliefs about others they think are lesser in some way is strong enough to lead them to bullying behavior. Bullies might be anti-Black racists, anti-Asian racists, Islamophobic, antisemitic, homophobic, or transphobic, or they might bully someone who is physically or mentally challenged. While some bullying is motivated by hate (i.e., based on prejudices and bias), and some is not, bullying and hate can be considered to be symbiotic:

- Like hate, bullying often involves harassment, intimidation, and discrimination.
- Bullying is about making someone feel small and powerless. Hate is about feeling superior to another group of people and wanting to deny them power and dignity.
- Bullying online (cyberbullying) can be considered a hate crime.

Behavior expert Barbara Coloroso informs us that people have got to be taught to discern what is right and to act on what they know is right. When we see someone ill-treating somebody and we think it's contemptible, it's because we've been taught that way. To help educators and parents understand what they might do to teach young people to think and act ethically, Barbara Coloroso often concludes by sharing how a Holocaust survivor responded to the question of what might have been done to prevent the atrocities:

- One: Pay attention.
- Two: Get involved.
- Three: Never look away.

When working towards stopping the hate and stopping the bullying, it matters that we give students the tools to use to stand up for their own rights while respecting the rights and legitimate needs of others, to handle conflicts non-violently, and to act with integrity when confronted with difficult situations of bullying, racism, and discrimination.

Two essential resources by Barbara Coloroso:
The Bully, The Bullied, and the Bystander. (2003) New York, NY: HarperCollins.
Just Because It's Not Wrong Doesn't Make It Right: Teaching Kids to Think and Act Ethically. (2012) Toronto, ON: Penguin Canada.

This collaboration between an educational researcher and a Grade 5 student helps shed light on the issues students are experiencing with body shaming and bullying in Ontario elementary schools. Over the last few years, Sophie (the student) has witnessed and experienced an increase in body shaming and body-shaming-related bullying in her school. The incident that inspired this piece is shared, followed by tips from Sophie about what information students and teachers need to make changes to school culture to create greater body positivity and more positive and inclusive school communities overall. Pseudonyms are used to protect the privacy of all involved.

PERSPECTIVE

A Case of Body Shaming/A Case of Bullying

by Steph Tuters and Sophie Stokkermans

Sophie
One day during recess, some friends were playing on the swings, and Karter called one of the girls in the class, Alexis ,"fat" and kicked her. Students started talking to each other rapidly, commenting on each other's appearance, and the conversation quickly escalated with more body shaming, with students making negative comments about each others' bodies and sizes. This kind of conversation was not new. Lately, there had been a lot of conversations during recess that involved body shaming and bullying. Just the day before, a few students had stood on chairs during in-door recess and yelled sexist comments at the girls, naming body parts and making negative comments about [the body parts] and the girls.

The bell rang, and everyone ran into the classroom. The information about the incident quickly spread to the rest of the class. People started chiming in and telling Alexis she was not fat and she was great just the way she was. Another student, Jaxon, spoke up and said they knew they are fat, as though it was something to be ashamed of. Grace turned to them and said she didn't think they should speak to themselves in a bad way, that everyone is a different size, and there's nothing wrong with that. Jaxon looked at Grace, considering what she was saying, but they didn't seem to believe her. Everyone stopped talking as the teacher entered the room.

What information do students need about body shaming?

- Students need their teachers to be aware of what students are talking about with each other, especially about their bodies.
- Students want teachers to educate them about how to like their bodies and not speak to themselves and each other in a mean way.
- Students need help learning how to have conversations with each other that are positive and affirming.
- Students need help learning how to stick up for one another if someone is being bullied or body-shamed.
- Students need help learning how to talk and think about bodies and body diversity in positive ways.

Steph

There is a lot of toxic information about bodies circulating in children's lives, with many children experiencing body-related bullying and body shaming. One in 10 children in Canada experience body shaming as a form of hate (Government of Canada, 2020). A study conducted in 2014 demonstrated that kids of all shapes and sizes experience body shaming and bullying about their bodies (Canadian Institute of Child Health, 2014). Children are exposed to negative conversations about bodies in many places: in person and online, in advertisements, on video games, by social media influencers, on television shows, and more. According to ETFO (2021), 31% of students experience cyberbullying, and 61% of it includes body shaming.

Some teachers (and parents) are intentionally avoiding conversations about bodies and body diversity, which leaves kids unprepared to understand and talk about their bodies in a positive way and counteract body shaming. Children are curious by nature: they see their bodies growing and changing, and they have questions. They need to have positive and supportive spaces where they can learn and ask questions.

The only way to change the narrative around bodies is to start to teach students how to stop this form of hate and treat each other and themselves with kindness, inclusivity, and respect.

See page 138 for references and resources.

Personal Narratives about Bullying

When we pose the question, "Have you or anyone you know experienced bullying?" there are sure to be stories popping up in the heads of our students—at any age. Statistics tell us that that each day more than 160 000 North American students miss school for fear of being bullied (National Education Association); that 58% of kids admit that someone has said something mean to them online (i-Safe America), and that one in four kids is abused by another youth (American Justice Department). The statistics about bullying incidents may vary from year to year, but they are irrefutable. Students have stories about bullies, being bullied, or being a bystander. Establishing a space where students feel comfortable to share these stories is important, not only for the storyteller who chooses to reveal their emotions, but also for those who listen and perhaps learn from these stories about ways to handle bullying.

Personal Stories about Bullying

I was a bully when I was nine or ten years old in public school. I remember pressing a girl, my age, up against a wall. A pack—a gang? a bunch?—of boys were behind me. I remember saying in a tough voice, "We don't like you cause you're fat." The bullied girl stared me down, squinched up her hand into a fist and whacked me on the centre of my head. I staggered. The boys quickly dispersed. I never bullied again.
— Lynn S.

I've been bullied at school for how I look. Some say all Asians look the same. They think it's easy to make fun of me by calling me names or saying my food smells weird or bad and more. Once I was opening my lunch and feeling excited to eat it. Then a girl across the table looked at me and said my food smelled horrible. That hateful comment made me lose my appetite.
— S.Y., Grade 6

My mother is Jewish. My father is not. When I was in Grade 7 a boy continued to torment me. When we were working on a group project, he insulted me by calling me a "Jew Boy." The teacher overheard this story and we both went down to the office. Nothing was done about this. A few weeks later, we were in gym class and the bully pushed me down on purpose and I got hurt. Eventually my parents got involved and let the principal and superintendent know that I was being bullied. I have no idea what was said or done to the bully. I did learn that it was so important to let others know what is happening to you and how hurt you can feel. I never got bullied in high school.
— Matt R.

Lesson: Assumptions

Discussion

Present the following statements to students to help them consider their views and assumptions about bullying. Working independently, students record whether they Strongly Agree (SA), Agree (A), Disagree (D), or Feel unsure (U). Students can then meet in small groups to share their responses and offer their perspectives about each statement.

1.	Most bullies have friends.	SA A	D	U
2.	There are as many boy bullies as girl bullies.	SA A	D	U
3.	Cyberbullying mostly happens outside school; it is not a school problem.	SA A	D	U
4.	Cyberbully messages are mostly filled with hate.	SA A	D	U
5.	Once a bully, always a bully.	SA A	D	U
6.	The best way to deal handle bullying is to report the problem to a teacher.	SA A	D	U
7.	Bullies generally think poorly about themselves.	SA A	D	U
8.	Bullies will go away if you ignore them.	SA A	D	U

Lesson: Cyberbullying

Discussion

Students work in pairs or small groups to discuss the *What if...* scenarios and consider solutions to each of the following:
- What if…you receive an email message spreading a nasty rumor about one of your friends?
- What if… you learn that your brother or sister has received a nasty email and asks you not to tell your parents?
- What if… you receive mean, hateful messages that, over a few weeks, get worse?
- What if… you and your best friend get into a fight and later you read mean comments they sent to others?

Lesson: Designing a Cover

Visual Arts

Tell students to imagine that they've been asked to create an illustration for the cover of a publication entitled *Stop the Bullying, Stop the Hate*. Students work independently to spontaneously prepare a sketch that they would offer the publisher to consider. Some students may choose to include figures, others may create a design that represents the bullying issue. Students can have the option of including speech bubbles or thought bubbles to their drawing.

As a follow-up, students share their images by discussing
- What story is being depicted in this scene?
- How successful did the illustration present a picture of a bully and/or a bullied and/or a bystander?
- Were male or female figures used to tell a story?
- What words if any might have been used to tell a story? What words might have been used to tell a story?
- How successfully were the emotions of each character conveyed?

Extension: Students can design a poster to publicize anti-bullying policies or provide contact information for someone who might need assistance in dealing with an issue.
- What image will be used to illustrate the message?
- What word will be included to catch someone's attention and to challenge them to confront the bully issue?

Lesson: Dramatizing Bullying

Drama

Provide an opportunity for groups to share their work a) with another group or b) with the whole class as audience. Invite students to discuss what is being shown in the scene. What is the story? What is the relationship between the characters? How does each character feel? How is issue of hate revealed in the dramatization?

1. Students work in groups of three to create a tableau scene entitled "I Hate You Because…" that can include bully, the bullied, and/or bystander(s). The activity can be repeated two additional times, with students switching roles.
2. Groups of three create an improvised story about hate in three still images, showing the beginning, middle, and end of the incident.

Extension: Students create a one-minute improvisation that brings the tableau story in step 2 to life. What might the characters be saying to each other? How will each character react to others? There should be no physical contact for this dramatization.

Lesson: Creating a Public Service Announcement

A Public Service Announcement (PSA) is an advertisement broadcast on radio, TV, or the internet for public interest. PSAs are intended to change attitudes by raising awareness about specific issues.

1. Students work in small groups to investigate one or more PSAs and then prepare a report to share with others.
2. Students work in groups to prepare a PSA for others to view. Decisions need to be made about whose point of view will be represented. Facts and information that have been gathered about the bullying epidemic can be shared in the PSA to convince others to think—and act—on behalf of those caught in the web of bullying and hate.

Bookshelf: Ten Essential Fiction Titles on Bullying

Titles are suitable for ages 9–13.

Blubber by Judy Blume

Egghead by Caroline Pignat

Loser by Jerry Spinelli

Real Friends by Shannon Hale; illus. LeUyen Pham (also *Best Friends; Friends Forever*)

Restart by Gordon Korman

The Reluctant Journal of Henry K. Larsen by Susin Nielsen

Starfish by Lisa Fipps

Wonder by R. J. Palacio (also *Auggie and Me: The Julian Chapter*)

Young Man with a Camera by Emil Sher; photography by David Wyman

Wolf Hollow by Lauren Wolk

Bookshelf: Resources on Bullying by Larry Swartz

The Bully, The Bullied, The Bystander, The Brave (Poems collected by David Booth and Larry Swartz)

The Bully-Go-Round: Literacy and Arts Strategies for Promoting Bully Awareness in the Classroom

Creating Caring Classrooms (with Kathleen Gould Lundy), Chapter 5: "Confronting the Bully Issue"

Dramathemes, 4th Edition, Chapter 5: "Confronting Bullying"

Drama Schemes, Themes & Dreams (with Debbie Nyman), Chapter 3: "The Bully Dance"

Teaching Tough Topics, Chapter 9: "Bullying"

6

Creating a Safer School Culture for All

"Our greatest glory is not in never failing, but in rising up every time we fail."
— Ralph Waldo Emmerson

"When they go low, we go high."
— Michelle Obama

"I alone cannot change the world, but I can cast a stone across the water to create many ripples."
— Mother Teresa

Text on pages 104–110 is written by Ardavan Eizadirad and Andrew Campbell.

Marginalized Population: A community of people who are disadvantaged and excluded from the mainstream based upon some aspect of their identity related to power and access to opportunities. (Sevelius et al., 2020)

Privilege: One group's access to something of value which is denied to other groups based on their identity. (McIntosh, 2003)

The world is progressing to become safer for diverse identities to be themselves in public spaces and feel a greater sense of belonging. With the creation of the #BlackLivesMatter movement in 2013 and increased support for Black, Indigenous, and People of Color (BIPOC) and other marginalized social groups, Western society is beginning to acknowledge how common systemic oppression can be for racialized populations (BBC, 2020; Eizadirad & Campbell, 2021; Matias, 2013). People and students who are invisibly diverse and systemically oppressed, such as queer, racialized, and neurodivergent individuals, are beginning to feel relatively safer in spaces that are inclusive—safer to share their authentic selves and who they are without masking key aspects of their identities (Herrmann, 2017; Kumashiro, 2004). In doing so, however, marginalized identities may experience bullying, hatred, intolerance, exclusion, and physical violence. Often those in positions of privilege and power have remained silent or failed to intervene to stop or reduce the harm. Without people speaking up or calling out harmful acts in educational spaces, whether physical in nature or indirect by denial of access to opportunities, systemic inequities are replicated, contributing to not meeting the needs of students and families in vulnerable conditions or circumstances.

By *systemic barriers*, we mean patterns and not exceptions. Hence, even though some students can overcome the challenges associated with growing up in a single-parent household or living in poverty, many families do not. We must ask how we can support marginalized students and families collectively by addressing the barriers they face in school and outside of school in the larger community. This is unique for each community and location. In many cases, those with higher socio-economic status and other dominant positions keep silent to avoid disrupting the conditions perpetuated—the status quo reaps them privilege. As Janaya Khan, the co-founder of Black Lives Matter Toronto, states, "Privilege isn't about what you've gone through. It's about what you haven't had to go through."

What Are Brave Spaces?

There are no spaces that are 100% safe for everyone. In other words, safe spaces do not exist (Campbell & Eizadirad, 2022). We must strive instead to advocate and create brave spaces where engagement in intentional risk-taking to support equity and social justice is encouraged (Arao & Clemens, 2013). Safe spaces encourage people to stay in the bubble of their comfort zone; brave spaces push individuals to come out of their comfort zone and engage in different perspectives and lived experiences different from their own (Campbell & Eizadirad, 2022). As educators, we hold the power and influence to elevate the diversity of perspectives presented in our classrooms and to facilitate conversations that might be uncomfortable, emotionally charged, or potentially triggering for some students. We should not avoid evoking emotions or feelings of discomfort in our classes, but rather be intentional about how we engage and deconstruct such teachable moments. This will contribute to the growth of all students as a community of learners and for minoritized students to shine and experience belonging.

The Shame of Silence

Silence can contribute to perpetuating harm by failing to stop or reduce the harm. Schools are prime institutions where a lack of commitment to equity and brave spaces can result in deafening silence or superficial performative politics (Ahmed, 2021); Kumashiro, 2004). This is the silence that allows hateful attitudes, such as thinking patterns rooted in stereotypical thinking, or racism and homophobia normalized through policies and practices, to continue (Hanna, 2019; Hooks, 2003). Our students might stay silent for fear of repercussions from their family and friends, workplaces, school, customs, and societal expectations.

Without active celebration of diversity and the questioning of normalized ideologies and practices in education, as well as a critical analysis of who it privileges and who it disadvantages and in what ways, our students learn they are not wanted for who they are and that they do not belong in such spaces. Silence prevents students from living and learning as their whole selves, policed by and shrouded in constant doubt, fear, and shame. This can replicate self-hatred and internal oppression. To create changes that allow our students to genuinely love who they are, we must unlearn harmful attitudes around difference, cultivate space for challenging and open dialogue, and advocate for the principles of humility, openness, acceptance, shared responsibility, reciprocity, and love in our classrooms. We have to be willing to model such behavior as educators and then expect it from our students as part of our classroom culture.

Check Yourself and Others

As you consider stories of hate, consider your own positionality and feelings around these issues. Before we can have crucial conversations with our students, we must have these conversations with our own selves and dig deep. Consider what types of conversations trigger your discomfort, fear, or defensiveness. Self-reflection and development of a critical consciousness is the first step towards courageous conversations with ourselves and our students. We often hope that these difficult conversations won't present themselves in our particular subject area, or that they can simply be avoided in the classroom. In classrooms with diverse students where authentic learning takes place, these conversations must come up in every subject area. Students can relate equity concepts to learning content or ask a related question, prompting a class discussion.

Even more important are the indirect comments that require crucial conversations to be addressed: the bully who whispers insults about the gay students at recess; the student who rolls their eyes at the gender-neutral bathrooms; the sarcastic and accusatory comments made under the class's breath when their neurodivergent classmate receives necessary accommodations on a test; the racialized students sitting together in an isolated corner of the lunchroom while the white students occupy most of the space and eat cafeteria lunches catered to their preferences. These scenarios show up in any subject, any grade, any school. Educators, administrators, students, and parents must choose be allies and advocate in solidarity for equity and social justice.

PERSPECTIVE

Using Your Power

by Ardavan Eizadirad

As educators, it is our responsibility to understand and acknowledge the hate around us in its different forms so that it can be challenged. Although students are young, they are far from ignorant or naive. Stories of hatred are splashed across their social media, televisions, and conversations. However, these stories of hate can fuel the fire of change rather than breed harm. Students understand the world around them, and real-world examples serve as concrete evidence for understanding and discussing issues of equity in classrooms. You have the power to address rather than ignore these issues and make a difference in students' perceptions and lives.

When preparing for the crucial conversations required to cultivate brave spaces, consider the resources you have available. Stories of hate can spark discussion, offer insight, and demonstrate the power of equity work and change. Find newspaper articles, case studies, research, and strong voices from minoritized identities to amplify in support of your conversation. Consider the sources of the knowledge you bring into the classroom. Whose lived experiences are presented and from what positionality?

Case Study: Music-Class Mocking
Michelle, a music teacher, is writing her end-of term-report cards at her desk while her students complete independent work. She notices that one of her students, Zara, hasn't handed in her last three assignments. Zara has always been an eager student and was recently identified as living with autism. Several weeks ago, one of Zara's peers began to mock her mannerisms and

Dr. Ardavan Eizadirad (@DrEizadirad) is an Assistant Professor in the Faculty of Education at Wilfrid Laurier University. Dr. Eizadirad is also the founder and Director of EDIcation Consulting (www. edication.org), which offers equity, diversity, and inclusion training to organizations.

See page 138 for references and resources.

stimming tendencies behind her back, imitating her movements while several of her classmates laughed on. Michelle had attempted to intervene by asking the student to stop, but several students had continued to make fun of Zara quietly over the past several weeks, especially when she plugged her ears during playing time and was unable to properly play her instrument. Michelle had noticed this but felt that the taunting was minor enough that she could let it slide. Zara couldn't see it happening, and it wasn't disrupting the class as a whole.

Michelle glances up from the report cards to look at the class and notices the taunting happening again: several of Zara's classmates mockingly plug their ears and chuckle to one another. Zara has moved away from her peers and is wearing noise-cancelling headphones in the back corner of the classroom. Michelle frowns at her report cards and wonders if the situation is worth addressing. Given Zara's diagnosis, Michelle does make accommodations for Zara; e.g., she doesn't expect Zara to hand everything in. But Michelle also doesn't want her students to get used to taunting someone. She considers how she might address the situation without expecting too much from Zara.

- How is stereotypical thinking influencing Michelle? What actions could she take to challenge this mindset and hold high expectations for all the students?
- What considerations and actions should be implemented to support Zara's success in the music classroom? Who should be involved and in what ways to resolve the matter?
- When have stereotypes or deficit thinking affected your ability to treat all students equitably? How has this limited your classroom in becoming a brave space?
- How could a more respectful classroom culture and a braver space be cultivated throughout the school year? What specific actions can alter the existing culture and create a more inclusive environment in the classroom?

Creating Brave Spaces

Creating brave spaces for learners does not happen overnight. It is a lifelong process that requires commitment and intentionality from everyone who contributes to the school climate, from students to parents, teachers, and administrators. Like any significant action, this process must begin with preparation and a clear plan. Creating brave spaces for students requires our courage to take a stand, make a difference, and substantially alter the status quo for the better. Preparation fosters courage by equipping us with the tools and ideas we need to take action, cementing our ideas to form a solid foundation. As a result, when unexpected or harmful situations arise, we feel more confident to address and engage with the parties involved to discuss them as teachable moments.

Preparation requires acknowledgment of student contexts and their unique identities, needs, and circumstances. Many students will never have been exposed to crucial conversations before. Some students may be shielded from these conversations at home by families who attempt to protect them or who have not acknowledged the inequities in the world themselves. For others, inequity and discrimination is a distinct piece of their lived experience, potentially leading to fear, defensiveness, and shutting down in a public conversation. Marginalized students might have witnessed their identities used as the punchline of a joke or the target of a bully's torment. Privileged students and staff can become defensive, preferring to maintain ignorance than to do the necessary work to create an equitable environment. These hurdles are not insurmountable, but must be accounted for in the planning phase of striving to create brave spaces in classrooms. Consider these questions:

- How will you react if your administrator denies the existence of racism at your school?
- What will you do if your students seem defensive or unreceptive to conversations about equity and social justice issues?
- How will you support students who might be triggered by such conversations? How will you introduce these conversations in a manner that is accessible to all students, with their unique backgrounds, contexts, identities, and lived experiences?
- How will you create inclusive spaces that value emotions and feelings being expressed instead of being perceived as a weakness?
- How can you create a brave classroom culture from the first day of school and onwards throughout the school year? Make a specific plan to carry this culture forward and consider the daily, weekly, and monthly actions and indicators to foster it.
- Is your classroom a brave space for students and colleagues to be their authentic selves? What signs of safety are demonstrated for them when they arrive? During their time in the class? Once they leave the space? Each of these components is a piece of their journey in your classroom that you hold the power to influence.

Pause and Reflect

For Educators

1. Consider the tools in your educator toolbox. What strategies do you use in your everyday lessons that could be applied to teaching about equity more effectively?
2. How can you account for your own identity and positionality when cultivating brave spaces? How can you get students to reflect their own positionality and lived experiences to gain more understanding about social issues?
3. Consider questions like the following:
   - If you are white, what considerations will you take to help your Black students know that they will be believed when they report experiencing racism?
   - If you are straight, what aspects of your classroom will empower your queer students?
   - How will you ensure that your lived experiences and identity serve to support all students?
   - What specific actions can you take to cultivate courage in yourself and your students and to integrate courageousness into the classroom culture?

For Students

1. Have you ever seen someone being bullied because of their differences or identity? How did you react? Is there anything you wish you had done differently to help create a braver space?
2. What are some ways you can talk about differences with others in your class to help create brave spaces and let everyone in the class know that they are celebrated, accepted, and welcome?
3. What supports do you need to feel that your classroom is a brave space? Make a plan to share these with a trusted teacher.
4. How will you intervene if you witness hate-based bullying at school?

For Administrators

1. What specific actions have you taken to normalize diversity in the workplace and support teacher and student safety? What policies and reporting procedures are in place to identify issues and prevent harmful acts? Does your staff understand what to do when they witness discrimination? Do they feel supported in taking actions against it?
2. How has your self-work influenced the ways you are able to lead? What resources, community organizations, and people are you consulting to help you grow in new ways? What inner work do you intend to do next to best support yourself, your staff, and your school to grow in new ways?

Breaking the Silence

We break the silence not simply by speaking, but also by standing up and acting. Silence begins when those in power choose to speak over marginalized voices or simply ignoring their needs and concerns. If you are an ally, you hold the power and privilege to change the narrative and hold space for diverse voices to speak up, be listened to, and build careers. If you are a person who has been silenced, how can you break the silence within yourself and begin to heal from the trauma you have endured?

We must show up with our whole selves to create brave spaces for students to discover their authentic selves and be proud of them (Hermann, 2017). What stories do you need to tell? What stories do you need to listen to? What is your truth, and how will you cultivate spaces that support the truths of your students? We must actively choose to do the necessary inner work to accept and love ourselves for who we are, including beliefs that we pass on to our students. As part of this process, it is important to find supportive groups to facilitate healing and taking collective action. Having a mentor will also drastically help you discuss challenging scenarios you come across during your teaching career. Allies have their own share of inner work to unpack their own assumptions and biases, as well as their own reinforcements of the dominant silencing culture. Through their positions of leadership, educators can serve as megaphones to amplify equitable conversations and support the necessary conditions for cultivating and maintaining brave spaces (Dixon, 2020).

> "Develop enough courage so that you can stand up for yourself and then stand up for somebody else."
> — Maya Angelou

"When the whole world is silent, even one voice becomes powerful."
— Malala Yousafzai

This chart outlines some of the many ways that everyone can contribute to inclusive classroom culture.

As an educator, you can…	As a student, you can…	As a marginalized voice, you can…
• Implement diverse curriculum that normalizes difference and teaches students about other cultures. • Encourage students to speak up and believe them when they tell you about harmful experiences. • Take immediate action, when you see discrimination, to undo the harm and consider what could be done to help prevent the situation from recurring.	• Seek to understand instead of criticizing. • Stand up for peers when they experience bullying or discrimination, rather than being a bystander. • Make space for friends and educators to speak up by being a supportive and active listener. • Ask teachers thoughtful questions about incorporating diversity into the classroom to create more inclusive spaces for everybody.	• Be bold and brave in standing up for yourself and others if you experience or witness discrimination. • Educate others, within your capacity, about ways to be respectful of diversity and why it is worth celebrating. • Research self-advocacy and ways that you can engage in it both in and out of school. • Be a role model for speaking up and breaking the silence.

No matter who you are, bravery for others involves cultivating classrooms in which challenging discussions are normalized, stereotypes and deficit thinking are challenged, and all are welcomed with love and support. We must take action to foster, create, and maintain brave spaces for every student and educator to create more inclusive classrooms.

PERSPECTIVE

Teaching Fairly in an Unfair World

by Kathleen Gould Lundy

The teacher's job in public education has always been about fairness. As we teach, we are intent on eliminating bias, preventing discrimination, and maintaining high expectations of excellence for every student who walks through the doors of our classrooms. Why do we strive so hard to make sure that teaching works and that learning matters? Because we want our students to get caught up in the full current of life—both in school and beyond—and to make good choices for the future. We want them to lead lives that are privately happy and publicly useful. We want them to grasp on to hope as they grow and learn, despite the difficulties that lie in their paths. In order for them to pursue a life worth living, they need to be resilient and positive.

Author of the book *Teaching Fairly in an Unfair World, 2nd edition*, Kathleen Gould Lundy is committed to creating inclusive classrooms where students feel safe to explore difficult issues and are challenged to become aware of what is fair, not only for themselves but also for others.

We teachers have enormous power to influence the future of the students in our care. We need to be mindful of that power and remain consistently conscious of what it means to teach fairly in an unfair world. Gaining students' trust and enlisting their cooperation are essential if we are going to succeed in the kind of critical work around social issues that is necessary in today's world.

We have to continually "check ourselves" by self-monitoring what we are saying, thinking, feeling, and doing in the classrooms and hallways of our schools. We need to be cognizant of our students' reactions and realities and know when to change direction, if necessary, while approaching tasks with sensitivity and discretion.

What Do Teachers Who Teach Fairly Do?

What are the characteristics and behaviors of a teacher who teaches fairly? Teachers who value and nurture a respectful classroom environment based on principles of fairness interact with their students in the following ways:

- They communicate ideas and instructions clearly.
- They guide and limit behavior to keep students safe.
- They expect all of their students to be successful.
- They encourage their students to be the best they can be on that particular day.
- They mentor their students in order to show them how to live in the world.
- They help students to question the construction and understanding of difference.
- They are open to new ideas and ways of approaching teaching and learning.
- They validate the experience of all their students by finding source material in the curriculum that acts as a mirror for the students' own identities.
- They engage students in critical thinking, by means of which they come to question and understand their relationships to their community, their society, and the world.
- They ensure that their students' needs, interests, and aspirations are met, not only through the curriculum, resources, pedagogy, and educational programs, but also through time spent together in the classroom.
- They help students examine their lives to understand their own personal histories.
- They listen and watch for those students who remain silent.
- They celebrate their students' successes.
- They know that learning takes time, so they rehearse and practice new skills.
- They "protect their students into understanding."
- They wear their profession in public.
- They view learning about teaching as never-ending.
- They value where their students are from, in terms of both their communities and the broader social context, and they remain mindful of that context so that teaching works and learning matters.

Promoting Healing, Hope, and Joy

The work we are all doing as leaders, as teachers, as students, and in the community to combat hate is powerful work. It is hard work, but we can also call it *heart* work. In a place where hate persists, we can shine our light. This light is powerful and comes from within us. Just as hate can spew out from within us, we can choose instead for love, joy, hope, and healing to emerge from us and out into the world.

One of the main ways we might do this is to ensure that we offer spaces of healing in our schools and communities. Many students have said that joining affinity spaces can be powerful to combat hate and discrimination. These spaces could include GSAs, Black or Asian affinity groups, or other spaces where community can be felt and healing can occur.

Allyship also holds significant value to healing. As educators, leaders, and students, we are more powerful than we know. We have the power to heal by being friends, being allies, standing up to bullies, speaking well of each other, and affirming each other. Healing looks different for different people, which gives us countless opportunities to support healing in our communities. We can also bring other people, professionals, and community resources into our schools to support healing on a regular basis. Consider the fact that when a hate crime is committed in a school or a shooting, the school board normally brings in professional counsellors to help the community heal. We have the power to implement this same support for the everyday hate we encounter.

Becoming an Activist

> "We ought to recognize that our greatest battle is not with one another but with our pain, our problems, and our flaws. To be hurt, yet forgive. To do wrong, but forgive yourself. To depart from this world leaving only love. This is the reason you walk."
> — Wab Kinew, Indigenous politician, author, media host

Ultimately, the work of disruption and stopping discrimination and hate involves encouraging each student to become an activist, someone who takes action against injustice. Activism is working to change the big problems in society, such as racism, classism, and other oppression. When embarking on activist initiatives, students might feel that they are not making a difference. But any steps that work towards dismantling racism and confronting hate help to make a positive change in society. Challenge students to think about what it means if they do nothing at all to make a difference. Students might feel uncomfortable, frustrated, or unsafe when choosing to become an activist. In most circumstances, activism does not mean working alone but involves working alongside like-minded others, people they can trust.

Being accountable is a large part of being an activist. Accountability means taking responsibility for ourselves. Remind students that they are in charge of what they say and do. Accountability also means recognizing that what we say and do has an effect on others. We need to help students be accountable for their words and actions, both negative and positive.

Lesson: How Can We Be Activists?

1. Have students work in groups to brainstorm different ways that they can be activists. Then, as a class, have students share their lists. Can the class come up with a list of 20 (or more) suggestions? Suggestions can be recorded.
2. Distribute or display the Actions to Take list on page 115.
3. Working alone, students review the list of suggested actions and place checkmarks beside 3 to 5 items they would feel most comfortable in trying.
4. Students meet in groups with three or four to share responses and discuss:

   - What is one personal goal you might take to become an activist?
   - Which item(s) have you practiced?
   - Which item(s) might be personally problematic?
   - Which item might you and your group collaborate on to take action?

Two books by Tiffany Jewell are significant resources for helping students think about activism: *The Antiracist Kid: A book about identity, justice and activism* and *This Book is Anti-Racist: 20 lessons on how to wake up, take action and do the work*

Lesson: Thinking about Taking Action (Group Discussion)

1. Students organize into groups of three or four, and each person is given a number.
2. Each #1 rolls a die. The number corresponds with these topics for the group to discuss:

   If you roll 1: Have you ever taken action to help someone in trouble? To stand up for a cause? Who were your supports? How did this make you feel?

   If you roll 2: Was there a time when you wish you had taken action but chose not to? Why didn't you? What might you learn from this experience?

   If you roll 3: Are you willing to go beyond your comfort zone to take action for a cause you believe in? What are some of the challenges of taking action?

   If you roll 4: Do you think that protesting a cause is worthwhile? Do protests help? What cause might you protest for?

   If you roll 5: American poet and activist Maya Angelou said, "When you know better, do better." What do these words mean to you? What are some ways in which someone can "do better"?

   If you roll 6: Do you think that hate can ever be stopped?

3. The person who rolled the die starts the discussion.
4. The conversation continues for about 2 minutes before the die is passed to person #2, who rolls the die for a new topic. If a person rolls the same number (i.e. the same topic), that person discusses that same topic from their point of view.
5. Group members are encouraged throughout to join in the conversation by asking questions or contributing a story or opinion.

Extensions

- This activity can be done without the roll of the die. Students meet in groups of four or five. Present this list of questions to the class:

  - Have you ever taken action to help someone in trouble? To stand up for a cause? Who were your supports? How did this make you feel?
  - Was there a time when you wish you had taken action but chose not to? Why didn't you? What might you learn from this experience?

- Are you willing to go beyond your comfort zone to take action for a cause you believe in? What are some of the challenges of taking action?
- Do you think that protesting a cause is worthwhile? Do protests help? What cause might you protest for?
- American poet and activist Maya Angelou said, "When you know better, do better." What do these words mean to you? What are some ways in which someone can "do better"?
- Do you think that hate can ever be stopped?

The group can discuss the questions and provide opinions, connections, and questions to each of the items they discuss. In a time limit of 15 to 20 minutes, students could have a chance to discuss all six topics.
- To reflect further on taking action, students can work independently to write a response to one of the questions above.

Actions to Take

☐ 1. Write persuasive letters to those who make rules and laws (in the community, in the country).

☐ 2. Boycott stores and businesses that have discriminated against others.

☐ 3. Start a group or club in the school: e.g., environmental club, anti-racist group, GSA, etc.

☐ 4. Participate in a protest, perhaps making protest sign to announce what you believe in.

☐ 5. Make your voice heard when you are concerned about an issue of discrimination that emerges in the classroom after reading a story, unpacking a news event, or exploring a theme or issue in any curriculum area.

☐ 6. Advocate for others. An advocate is someone who supports others by sharing their power, speaking up, arguing, and promoting a cause.

☐ 7. Read a novel that has racism, bullying, or homophobia present in the narrative. Share your reactions with others in writing or through discussion.

☐ 8. Read about heroes, living or dead, young or old, who have resisted discrimination and other forms of microaggressions. What can we learn from the activism of others?

☐ 9. Choose an activist hero to admire. What actions did they take? Why? How did they persevere in the face of adversity? Amplify their words, ideas, and actions.

☐ 10. Learn the language and gain knowledge about the vocabulary of discrimination. Investigate definitions that can help foster understanding.

☐ 11. Pay attention to the news. Bring stories of hate that are featured almost daily in the media. Participate in a discussion where different viewpoints from classmates are heard.

☐ 12. Share your personal stories about injustices.

☐ 13. Report any cyberbullying or hate messages you've witnessed on social media.

☐ 14. Take action by making art. Create a poster. Create a dramatization. Create a Public Service Announcement (PSA).

☐ 15. Have discussions at home about incidents of injustice you have witnessed.

☐ 16. Even when you think no one will pay attention, let your anti-hate voice be heard.

☐ 17. Listen to the stories of others in your world.

☐ 18. Seek help if you have been the victim. It is not your fault. Confiding in others is an important step for supporting and acting on hate experiences.

☐ 19. Share what you know about racism and other forms of discrimination. Learn facts. Investigate statistics. Seek and tell the truth. Talk about what is fair and just when talking about injustice.

☐ 20. Be kind.

Pembroke Publishers ©2023 *Stop the Hate for Goodness Sake* by Andrew Campbell and Larry Swartz ISBN 958-1-55138-358-3

7

Ten Tips for Disrupting Hate

Tip 1: Uncover Your Unconscious Biases

"Stopping our racist patterns must be more important than working to convince others that we don't have them."
— Robin DiAngelo (2016)

This is one of the most important aspects of disrupting hate for teachers to address because we all have unconscious biases. As educators and individuals, if we leave our unconscious biases unchecked, uncovered, or unattended to, we will make further assumptions, strengthen stereotypes and images of hate, and approach our students with deficit thinking. This, in turn, will often harm already marginalized groups of students in our classrooms, programs, and decision-making. The process involves understanding what our unconscious biases are, how we can uncover them, and how we can dismantle them to grow as culturally competent educators.

An unconscious bias is a prejudiced or unsupported judgment in favor of or against one thing, person, or group compared to another. These biases occur automatically, as the brain makes quick judgments based on our past experiences and background. As a result of these unconscious biases, certain people benefit while others are penalized. Consider who benefits when an interview panel is made up of eight middle-class white women and they are interviewing a tall Black Caribbean man with a Jamaican accent. Who benefits and who is penalized when durags and loc hairstyles and headwraps are disallowed in school dress codes?

How do our unconscious biases show up in our school culture and climate? Whose pictures are on the wall; what does the school look like; what practices are at play in the classroom? How do these biases show up in our classrooms and our lessons? We perceive students and their backgrounds, our school, and our community neighborhood, and we act based on these perceptions. We want to ensure that our actions are inclusive and do not further marginalize our students.

Unconscious biases can be changed, broken down, and eliminated if we choose to intentionally work on them.

Develop Your Toolbox

- We all make assumptions and act on them in schools, so we must be very careful about the biases we hold. The journey begins by gaining awareness of our unconscious biases and understanding that they affect how we teach, plan, and operate.
- We must educate ourselves on unconscious bias, ask questions, and develop safe and brave spaces for conversations to be had about the biases we hold in our schools, homes, and everyday life.

Act On It

Challenge your students to question the traditional assumptions made about Black students, gay students, students in wheelchairs, and students who are hard of hearing. Let's engage in self-reflection by questioning our privilege and its influence, learning from our experience, maintaining an open mind, and practicing empathy. Through a growth mindset, we can come to a place where we are bold enough, brave enough, equipped enough, and adaptable enough that we can break down our unconscious biases to be better educators.

Tip 2: Change Your Mindset

> "To bring about change, you must not be afraid to take the first step. We will fail when we fail to try. Each and every one of us can make a difference."
> — Rosa Parks (2008)

As we begin the work of equity, diversity, inclusion, belonging, anti-racism, and anti-hate, it is crucial to consider our mindset towards learning and unlearning. For years, I have seen people question why they need to learn something new, why they need to unlearn something they have worked with for years, and why every day there is something new to unpack when it comes to inclusion work.

When it comes to learning, we are often inclined to push back at equity work. Think about any occupation or skill and consider how that industry, program, and content has changed over the years. There are things that I did and learned about as a young teacher that would never be used today. Years ago, we were big on differentiation and universal design for learning, which we have now moved beyond. I also remember the first time I heard the word *queer*. Even as a member of the LGBTQ+ community, I had never used the word *queer* in my community; now it is a word we use regularly. New words such as *intersex* and *two-spirit* have been introduced to our vocabulary, as more identities are recognized and important conversations are had.

Develop Your Toolbox

- We must be open to learning. Our mindset is part of the problem when it comes to equity work. Rather than calling out educators, this is an invitation to be called in.
- Our mindsets of "this is too much" or "here we go again," or questioning why we need to learn another word or another letter or a new pronoun, can cause

real harm and further perpetuate hate. These mindsets of not wanting to learn are a significant part of the problem.

Act On It

If we remove the issues of equity, we will realize how often we are excited to learn for our next promotion or next job, how much we look forward to gaining skills and tools. Yet somehow, when it comes to equity work, we often have issues with moving forward. We must recognize our privilege and take a step back to stop, correct our mindset, and move forward with inclusion at the forefront of our learning.

Tip 3: Develop Culturally Relevant and Responsive Pedagogy

"Abolitionist teaching starts with freedom dreaming, dreams grounded in a critique of injustice. These dreams are not whimsical, unattainable daydreams, they are critical and imaginative dreams of collective resistance." (Love, 2019, p. 101)

Teachers and teacher candidates must have a wide range of tools in our toolboxes to work together against hate. Making space for culturally responsive and relevant pedagogy is a vital first step. As the faces in our classrooms change, our practice, our planning, and our teaching must all be guided by culturally responsive and relevant pedagogy to support and celebrate this growing diversity. This is not something that can be tacked on at the end of a list or added because we have a racialized student or a queer student. It must be embedded into our entire practice and everything we do. It is planning, practice, and pedagogy.

Culturally responsive teaching is a pedagogy that recognizes the importance of including students' cultural references in all aspects of learning. When the examples from which we teach are completely irrelevant or unrelatable for students, we need to take students from an unknown place to the known. Our students do not come to school as blank slates. They come from homes, parents, practices, religions, foods, and countries. These are all topics that can be brought into the classroom to openly discuss culture and the appropriate responses to hate. We must make the effort to understand our students and help them feel as though we see them.

Teaching is 40% content and 60% engagement, and we need to ensure that our students feel a sense of belonging in our classrooms. Where do they see themselves in the examples being taught, in what is posted on the walls? Where is the room for student self-expression and identity to be prominently featured during class? Teaching must integrate a student's background, identity, voices, knowledge, and community experiences into curriculum. Our students must be seen and must understand that who they are matters.

Develop Your Toolbox

Consider how you discuss people who are different from you. Do you talk about refugees in a deficit way or through a stereotyped definition? Do you hear conversations about your students on the spectrum being a burden rather than treated with high expectations, dignity, humanity, and love?

Choose to incorporate diverse families, races, abilities, and cultures into your teaching, resources, and lesson planning. Equity and anti-hate begin from the inside out. We can choose to be part of the magic, not part of the mess, through culturally relevant and responsive pedagogy.

Tip 4: Become a Champion for Inclusion

> "If we want to achieve our goal, then let us empower ourselves with the weapon of knowledge and let us shield ourselves with unity and togetherness."
> — Malala Yousafzai (2013)

When we think about diversity and inclusion, we must consider our students: the people who might be excluded, pushed aside and not brought to the forefront. Our role as educators and advocates is to be the champion our students need. Students need people who will be there for them, speak on their behalf, ensure that they are included, and make sure that things they need are provided.

The first thing we must do as champions for our students is to evaluate personal biases and prejudices that have influenced our view and understanding of otherness and hate. We might begin to do the work of inclusion, but how we see difference and inclusion requires taking the time to unpack who we are and examine our own biases, positionality, history, and experiences. We must ensure that self-reflection and proper engagement allow us to properly unpack stereotypes and unconscious biases that affect our own perceptions and work against our efforts to create a more inclusive and equitable school environment.

It is also important that we are prepared to identify the patterns of discrimination, inequality, and injustice in our communities and to find tangible ways to address them. We might not know what access looks like or what having access denied looks like in our schools, which are signs that we, as champions, must learn to recognize.

In addition to self-awareness and the awareness of others, we must create access to opportunities. We cannot be stuck with the idea of checking a box or creating a policy on paper if we do not have meaningful and intentional action behind it. For those of us who are from privileged spaces, how can we use that power, privilege, and access to create opportunities for others? How are we taking the time to understand who our students really are and the contexts they bring?

Develop Your Toolbox

- As a champion, is it important to take time to understand what we are passionate about, what our advocacy is about, and who our students are. How do we create the necessary awareness, access, engagement, and opportunity for students to ensure that they have what they need to be amazing?
- As teachers, we can walk into the classroom and truly listen to our students to create access. We can make sure that our students see themselves around the classroom by allowing them to share, by taking down the posters we have traditionally used and putting up students' voices and creativity in their place, by hearing stories about their days, and by letting students see themselves reflected in all aspects of their learning.

Act On It

Making opportunity might look like taking time to speak to the principal to ask for more technology or creating fundraisers so that all children have access. Some schools will be equipped with software and devices, while others might be like a desert for technology, with very little that their students can access. We need champions in our schools for the students who are disenfranchised, marginalized, and excluded. We need our champions to speak up, speak out, and act. We want our students coming home to say, "I went to school today, and I was engaged. My teacher saw me, and I had an amazing day." This is the power of a champion.

Tip 5: Disrupt the Deficit Mentality

> "[Deficit thinking is] a very common way of thinking which affects our general way of being in and constructing the world. Differences from the 'norm' are immediately seen as being deprived, negative, and disadvantaged. It never questions the legitimacy of what is deemed to be normal, nor does it consider that differences may actually go beyond expected norms. It discourages teachers and administrators from recognizing the positive values of certain abilities, dispositions, and actions." (Sharma, 2016)

Hateful stereotypes and assumptions are born from deficit mentalities, which most significantly harm our most marginalized students. As we work together to combat hate in schools, how do we ensure that our approaches are strength-based rather than stemming from deficit thinking? Our approaches must come from a language of hope and a place of strength. This mentality is supported by the intentional selection of strength-based resources, videos, and language in our classrooms.

 When I taught in Atlanta back in 2000, my students asked me questions about my experiences in Jamaica. These students asked some questions that were shocking: Did I live in a treehouse? Did I catch my own food at the beach each day? Did I know Bob Marley? While these questions stem from deficit assumptions and stereotyping, what these students simply wanted to do was share information that they considered fact — based on their exposure to conversations about Jamaica. — Andrew Campbell

Deficit thinking is rooted in blame and shame of difference. Differences can, in fact, surpass expected norms, making space for creativity, diversity, and unique joy. Consider an ESL student who does not speak Canadian English but has mastered three other languages, and who holds a unique and multiculturally informed worldview as a result. An advantage for this student can be shut down by deficit thinking if we limit ourselves to seeing only the student's lack of English experience.

Develop Your Toolbox
- We must be curious about the stories we tell ourselves about attendance, late arrivals, and learning accommodations. Framing these things through a deficit lens creates real danger for hate and stereotyping to arise for our students, as it discourages teachers from recognizing the positive value of certain

120

differences and encourages viewing our students through a one-dimensional lens.

- Culturally relevant and responsive pedagogy is not about a book with a Black girl, a First Nations person, or a person in a wheelchair on the cover. It is about holding high expectations for students, seeing their different abilities, and valuing what they bring to school. Deficit thinking is rooted in a need to fix individuals, rather than recognizing that what truly needs fixing is the system that prevents our students from thriving as their unique, authentic, and best selves.

Act On It

We must go beyond our default assumptions that all people are the same and recognize the intersectionalities that shape who our students are. We must choose to pack our toolboxes with strength-based approaches that do not marginalize our students based on misinformation and misconstructions. Continue to be mindful, engaged, and self-reflective to grow your equity journey and move beyond deficit thinking.

Tip 6: Cultivate the Language of Hope

> "Don't ever underestimate the impact you can have, because history has shown us that courage can be contagious, and hope can take on a life of its own."
> — Michelle Obama (2011)

When moving from deficit to strength-based approaches, the language we use to talk about our students makes an enormous difference in supporting strength and reducing hate. Many teachers will overhear conversations by other teachers in staff rooms, in classrooms, and in their lives that are indicative of deficit thinking. This may involve holding low student expectations, putting down the class, or even making borderline rude comments to the students who are most in need of support and care. Our presence in a classroom, the way we approach our students, and the energy we bring into the room is just as much a part of culturally relevant and responsive pedagogy as any formal strategy from an academic journal. A teacher's presence, smile, heart, and morning greeting have an enormous impact on students by enhancing love, joy, and safety in the classroom.

 I recall wondering how to speak to students about frequent absences many years ago. I could accuse them of staying away, being frequently ill, or of not wanting to engage, or I could choose to approach it differently. When my students returned, I could welcome them back with open arms and tell them that I missed them. I could explain what they missed and tell them that we will work together to get the work done. This approach is a choice of strength over deficit and of love over hate.
— Andrew Campbell

We must remember that no two of our students are the same, even those who share common identities. Not all of our racialized students are the same, not all of our queer students are the same, and not all of our refugee students are the same. Each one of our students is vibrant, unique, and deserving of care and love for who they are. We must see our students as individuals; one size does not fit all. Diversity offers us hope for the future and for the myriad strengths with which it equips our students. We must focus on our language through the lens of hope and recognize that students' needs and differences are not shortcomings, but opportunities for them.

Develop Your Toolbox
- Take a moment to consider the strength-based language being used in your school from your principal, colleagues, and students.
- Each time you hear language that is rooted in hope and strength-based thinking and moving away from hate, take note of it and add it to your toolbox. We can demonstrate disruption through radical love, curriculum improvements, speaking up, and calling in.

Act On It
By using the language of hope and becoming, we begin to destroy and dismantle attitudes and actions of hate. We can choose to care about our students with intentionality and prioritize strength-based approaches, and it is rooted in the words we use.

Tip 7: Care for Students

> "There is a tribe in Africa called Masai whose traditional greeting to each other is 'Casserian Engeri'. It means, 'And how are the children?' They do not ask each other, 'How are you?' or 'How's your day?' but rather they ask about the next generation. The Masai believe that monitoring the well-being of their children is the best way to determine the future health and prosperity of their whole society." (The Hunt Institute, 2016)

The fabled African Masai tribe was considered to have the most fearsome, mighty, and intelligent warriors. In all that we do as warriors—the fighting, the defending—the most important thing is always to remember the children in our care and honestly ask how they are. When we walk into any classroom, we must see our students, create a sense of belonging, show love, and teach every student with the enormous love, respect, and passion that they deserve. Consider: how are the children? There is a duty of care to which we must commit as educators. When we do the work of equity, diversity, and inclusion, the work of anti-Black racism, and the work of anti-discrimination, what is our end goal? As educators, we are all striving to support each one of the children in our care when we do the work of disrupting deficit thinking in our schools. All children deserve our protection and care.

Develop Your Toolbox
- As we enter new schools, many of us may be placed in communities of which we are not a member. This is an opportunity for us to sit in a space of humility and to learn from our brilliant students about how to become better educators and a more culturally competent human beings.
- When you are asked, "How are the children," will you be able to truthfully and thoughtfully respond that the children are well?

Act On It

Our children will be well, not because we are perfect educators, but because we use intentionality to create spaces of belonging, an inclusive classroom culture, a disruption of hurt, words of hope and positivity, and a classroom filled with genuine care. We might meet teachers who are tired, negative, and feeling powerless, but we must always remember the power that we hold to change a child's life through care, love, and joy, and to disrupt the hate they might encounter.

Tip 8: Ask Yourself, "Who Am I Teaching?"

"In diversity there is beauty and there is strength."
— Maya Angelou (*The Root*, 2014)

When we prepare a lesson plan, we can consider how we are teaching, what we are teaching, and how we will know whether our students understood the lesson. Let us also consider *who* we are teaching. Every time we begin a lesson plan, we must take a moment to be conscious of the students in front of us. This involves being conscious of not only the curriculum topics and sub-topics, but also how these topics are best taught to this particular set of learners.

 Growing up in Jamaica, I remember teaching reading to a room full of boys. A few weeks into teaching, it clicked! The stories I was using were not of interest to these students, as I was using storybooks that were recommended to me as a very young teacher. Many of these students were interested in sports and cars, but the books I had to offer them were fairy tales and stories to which they struggled to relate. I remember trying my best to gather different books and using my own money to purchase new books, because I now understood that in front of me were boys who wanted to read about cars. I began with their interests and planned my lessons, activities, and materials from there. — Andrew Campbell

We are going to enter classrooms where the students are from different spaces, are in different places, and have a wide range of different experiences. We must consider how we will teach all students in a way that supports their unique lives and backgrounds. Consider giving a monkey, an elephant, a snake, and a dog the same task for evaluation: to climb a tree. This text is given to all participants in the same style and format, when each of them have varied abilities, learning styles, capabilities, and interests. Comparing a monkey's ability to climb a tree versus an elephant's is just as ridiculous as expecting two learners to succeed in exactly the same way.

The opportunity to observe experienced educators is a privilege we can never take for granted. Consider how your colleagues listen to and have conversations with their students. Think of the students who are taking, who are not sharing, whose hands are always up, who are always by themselves, and use these observations to learn how to build relationships and trust with students. Once you have taken the time to get to know your students, you can begin making intentional choices about lesson planning. Some of these considerations should involve whose voices are represented by the stories we bring into the classroom, whose perspectives are being featured in visuals, and how our lesson plans can reflect a broader range of experiences.

- How will we create space for student voice? We have introductory tools from our teacher education programs, but we ultimately learn to teach while actively teaching.
- We must be mindful when creating representations of other cultures to encourage respect, authenticity, and care.

Act On It

We have many resources at our disposal that can help us be amazing educators—if we are aware, intentional, and mindful towards them. Whose voices and perspectives are being seen in our classes? Can our students say that they saw themselves in our lessons, on our walls, in our media? To truly fight hate, our students must see themselves in all of the things we do.

Tip 9: Move from Awareness to Action

"In a racist society, it is not enough to be non-racist. We must be anti-racist."
— Angela Davis (The Buffalo Center for Health Equity, 2022)

As educators, it is our responsibility to know others on a broader scale than our neighborhoods and school communities. We must be aware of the many global issues of hate surrounding us that could be affecting our students. Our work as educators is to look at definitions, terminologies, data, trends, and expert voices to gain awareness of difference and to actively fight back against hate.

Some educators may be willing to name, share, speak up, and talk about barriers faced by immigrant, ESL, and Black students in the classroom and on the playground. These people have seen exclusion and disenfranchisement in schools, understand inequities, and are willing to engage in courageous conversations. However, there are also people who refuse to acknowledge the issues, and this supports and maintains the issues. Refusing to acknowledge barriers communicates that any intention to disrupt and make change is inauthentic. This consistently centres the feelings of the privileged over the feelings of those who are already marginalized.

We must not make the mistakes of maintaining deficit mentalities, holding low expectations for racialized students, and giving off subtle messages that clearly tell children they do not belong. The impact of such practices as streaming and low representation are damaging to students and can perpetuate the very hate we aspire to eradicate. We ask our educators to be changemakers, to understand what systemic racism looks like and its impact on education, and to help chart a better way forward. We are faced by problems caused by hidden institutional biases in policies, practices, and processes, and we can solve these problems only by actively and intentionally practicing greater awareness. We must look around ourselves and question: who is being hired, who sits on boards and committees, what do policies and books say, and who has access?

Develop Your Toolbox

- If just one teacher in a school is intentionally deliberate about who is represented in the curriculum, stories, and images in the classroom, this can spark change and reduce hate.

- If identities and community are honored by just one teacher in the building, that magic spreads until a dozen teachers follow suit.

Act On It

Imagine how much safer our schools would be if we acknowledged and disrupted hatred, if we admitted that residential schools were a crime scene, if we stopped checking boxes to meet standards and instead acted with humility, care, love, and awareness.

Tip 10: Develop Solidarity and Allyship

"Allyship is not self-defined—our work and our efforts must be recognized by the people we seek to ally ourselves with."
— Layla Saad (2022)

It is critical for white educators to intentionally show solidarity with racialized groups. However, it is also important for BIPOC educators to show cross-racial solidarity to promote equity and inclusion. While it can be lonely to be one of the few racialized educators in a particular school, there are community spaces and affinity groups in which BIPOC educators can feel nurtured, find a sense of belonging, and stand in solidarity. Unless we stand shoulder to shoulder and fight against all forms of oppression, we will not be able to effectively dismantle any form of racism.

We cannot separate anti-hate work into Black Lives Matter initiatives one day, Stop Asian Hate the next, and decolonization another. To fully understand the root cause of racism, oppression, and colonization is to understand white supremacy as the foundation. This could be through intergenerational wealth or socio-cultural capital, both manifesting as unearned privilege. Look at the wealthiest people in our world: Jeff Bezos, Elon Musk, Bill Gates, Mark Zuckerberg. There is a clear common identity among people in power who have the authority to make decisions. Equity cannot be achieved until positions of power represent true diversity. This is distinct from tokenism, where a single Black or Indigenous person is included, simply to check a box. BIPOC people, who are operating from an equity framework and bring lived experiences of marginalization to the table, must fill seats of power. We must critically analyze the imbalance of power at each institution and make greater strides towards enabling BIPOC folks to gain this power. We can do this by all working together, fighting for one another, and elevating all races and groups.

Develop Your Toolbox

- White educators must believe the stories of racialized students, educators, and administration, and must hold space for healing.
- Just because a white teacher reaches out to someone racialized with a positive intention, that teacher cannot self-label as an ally without action behind it. BIPOC people provide the label of *ally* through witnessing interactions, authenticity, and sincerity that goes beyond performativity and hashtags.

Act On It

It is possible to disrupt hate through empathy, love, nurturing, and belonging. We must all build genuine relationships with one another, both in and out of

See page 127 for keys to stopping the hate in an alphabet acrostic to display and share.

schools, which are rooted in support, care, and healing. We must listen to the vulnerable sharing of BIPOC folks and validate their stories, suffering, and joy. Creating safer spaces in this way leads to more inclusive classrooms, braver conversations, and more authentic opportunities for allyship.

Acknowledge the HATE

Brave the HATE

Confront the HATE

Disrupt the HATE

Erase the HATE

For

Goodness Sake,

STOP THE HATE!

Glossary

Activism: policy or direct action that uses vigorous campaigning to bring about political or social change

Agency : the power to make effective change; ability to make choices and decisions

Assimilate: to take in the customs and mannerisms and ideas of a dominant group

Bias: a personal preference, for or against, towards an individual or group. A bias attitude can interfere with judgment.

Bigot: a person who is unreasonably attached to a belief or opinion, particularly when prejudiced against or antagonistic toward others

BIPOC: Black, Indigenous, People of Colour

Cisgender: when gender identity (how you identify) is the same as your sex (your physical form)

Colonize: when group of settlers establish political control over the indigenous people of the area

Democracy: a government run by the people. Each citizen has a say (a vote) in how the country is run

Discrimination: when thoughts or actions favor one group over another; the unjust treatment of people who have different opinions than yours

Deficit thinking: the idea that students from various "at risk" groups fail in school due to such factors as home life, economic status, gender, and race

Equality: when each individual or group of people is given the same resources and opportunities

Equity: the quality of being fair and impartial; recognizes that each person has different circumstances that accounts for specific disadvantages

Ethnicity: refers to cultural factors including nationality, regional culture, ancestry, and language

Freedom: the power or right to act, speak, or think as one wants without hindrance or restraint

Gender identity: a personal sense of who you are, which may or may not be the same as the sex assigned at birth

Harassment: actions—aggressive pressure; intimidation; unwanted behavior physical or verbal (or suggested)—that make a person feel uncomfortable, humiliated, or distressed

Intersectionality: the interconnected nature of social categories, such as race, class, and gender, as they apply to a given individual or group; how a person's social and political identities combine to create discrimination and privilege

Justice: giving each person what they deserve; fairness

Kindness: the quality of being friendly, generous, and considerate

LGBTQ2S+: sexual orientations and gender identities that aren't heterosexual or cisgender: Lesbian, Gay, Bisexual, Transgender, Queer or Questioning, Two-Spirit, plus others

Marginalized: to be on the outside of a dominant culture and treated as if you are insignificant or inferior

Microaggression: a statement, action, or incident regarded as an instance of indirect or subtle but intentional discrimination against members of a marginalized group

Nazism: a fascist party requiring supreme devotion to the German government (The Third Reich) 1933–1945

Oppression: the systemic suppression of a group or groups; when one group of people believe they are better than another and abuse and misuse their power against the second group

Prejudice: a preconceived opinion or feeling, which can be favorable or unfavorable; unreasonable feelings, opinions, or attitudes especially hostile to racial, social or religious group

Privilege: the benefits, advantages, and power due to the social identities of a dominant culture

Queer: an umbrella term for people who are not heterosexual or cisgender

Race: one of the major groups into which human beings can be defined according to their physical characteristics, such as bone structure and skin, hair, and eye color; groups of people who have similarities in biological traits deemed by society to be socially significant

Racism: prejudice, discrimination, or antagonism directed against someone of a different race, based on the belief that one's own race is superior

Racist: a person who shows or feels discrimination or prejudice against people of other races, or who believes that a particular race is superior to another

Slur: an insinuation about someone that is intended to insult them or damage their reputation

Stereotype: a common, simplified, or distorted view of a person, thing, or group that is not based on fact

Swastika: an ancient religious and cultural symbol that appeared in various Eurasian, African, and American cultures; the swastika is widely recognized for its appropriation by the Nazi party and neo-Nazis

Transgender: someone who's gender identity differs from the gender they were assigned at birth

Upstanders: individuals who recognize that bullying or hate are wrong and act to make a given situation right; those who strive to give support to and protect the bullied and those who are discriminated against

White Supremacy: the belief that white people, because they are white, are superior to Black, Brown, Indigenous, and other global majorities

Woke: being alert to injustice in society, especially racism

Xenophobia: dislike or prejudice against people from other countries

Youth Activism: the participation of teenagers and young adults in organizing for social change

Zealot: a person who is fanatical and unwilling to make compromises in pursuit of religious or political ideals

Dr. Larry Recommends

Picture Books: Inclusion ABC

All Are Welcome by Alexandra Penfold; illus. Suzanne Kaufman
All Because You Matter by Tami Charles; illus. Bryan Collier
Be You by Peter H. Reynolds
The Boy, The Mole, The Fox and the Horse by Charlie Mackesy
The Day You Begin by Jacqueline Woodson; illus. Rafael López
EveryBody's Different on EveryBody Street by Sheree Fitch; illus. Emma Fitzgerald
I Am Every Good Thing by Derrick Barnes; illus. Gordon C. James
I Am Human: A book of empathy by Susan Verde; illus. Peter H. Reynolds
I Promise by LeBron James; illus. Niña Mata
I Wish You Knew by Jackie Azúa Kramer; illus. Magdalena Mora
Inclusion Alphabet: ABC's for everyone by Kathryn Jenkins
Intersection Allies: We Make Room for All by Chelsea Johnson, LaToya Council & Carolyn Choi; illus. Ashley Seil Smith
A Kid Is a Kid Is a Kid by Sara O'Leary; illus. Qin Leng
Most People by Michael Leannah; illus. Jennifer E. Morris
My Skin Your Skin: Let's talk about race, racism and empowerment by Laura Henry-Allain; illus. Onyinye Iwu
Same, Same But Different by Jenny Sue Kostecki-Shaw
This is a School by John Schu; illus. Veronica Miller Jamison
We Are All Wonders by R.J. Palacio
Whoever You Are by Mem Fox; illus. Leslie Staub
You Are Enough Margaret O'Hair; illus. Sofia Cardoso
You Matter by Christian Robinson

Fiction: Twenty Essential Titles

For ages 9–13

Answers in the Pages by David Levithan (homophobia)
A Place to Belong by Cynthia Kadohata (anti-Asian racism)
Borders by Thomas King; illus. Natasha Donovan (graphic text) (anti-Indigenous Racism)
Broken Strings by Kathy Kacer and Eric Walters (antisemitism)
Count Me In by Varsha Bajaj (Islamophobia)
Flying Over Water by Shannon Hitchcock & N.H. Senzai (Islamophobia)
Ghost Boys by Jewell Parker Rhodes (anti-Black racism)
Jennifer Chan is Not Alone by Tae Keller (bullying)
Linked by Gordon Korman (antisemitism)
Look Both Ways: a tale told in 10 blocks by Jason Reynolds (anti-Black racism)
The Many Meanings of Meilan by Andrea Wang (anti-Asian racism)
New From Here by Kelly Yang (anti-Asian racism)
On the Line by Paul Coccia and Eric Walters (homophobia)

Prairie Lotus by Linda Sue Park (anti-Asian racism)
Restart by Gordon Korman (bullying)
Rick by Alex Gino (also *Melissa*) (homophobia)
Wishtree by Katherine Applegate (Islamophobia)
Yusuf Azeem is not a Hero by Saadia Faruqi (Islamophobia)]

YA Fiction

Ages 13+

The Door of No Return (trilogy) by Kwame Alexander (free verse novel) (anti-Black Racism)
Felix Ever After by Kacen Callender (also *King and the Dragonflies*) (homophobia)
The Good War by Todd Strasser (antisemitism)
The Hate U Give by Angie Thomas (prequel: *Concrete Rose*) (anti-Black racism)
Last Night at the Telegraph Club by Malinda Lo (homophobia)
Long Way Down by Jason Reynolds (also *Long Way Down*, graphic novel with art by Danica Novgorodoff) (anti-Black racism)
Some Kind of Hate by Sarah Darer Littman (racism)
Parachutes by Kelly Yang (anti-Asian racism)
Under the Iron Bridge by Kathy Kacer (antisemitism)
What We're Scared Of by Keren David (antisemitism)

True Stories: Biographies, Memoirs

All Boys Aren't Blue (memoir) by George M. Johnson (YA) (homophobia)
Brown Girl Dreaming by Jacqueline Woodson (anti-Black racism)
Diary of a Young Girl by Anne Frank (antisemitism)
Everything Sad Is Untrue (a true story) by Daniel Nayeri (Islamophobia)
Fatty Legs by Christy Jordan-Fenton & Margaret-Olemaun Pokiak-Fenton; illus. Liz Amini-Holmes (sequel: *A Stranger at Home*) (anti-Indigenous racism)
New Kid by Jerry Craft (graphic text) (sequels: *Class Act; School Trip*) (anti-Black racism)
Viola Desmond Won't Be Budged (picture book) by Jody Nyasha Warner; illus. Richard Rudnicki (anti-Black racism)

Nonfiction

All About Anne from the Anne Frank House
The Anti-Racist Kid: A book about Identity, Justice and Activism by Tiffany Jewell; illus. Nicole Miles
How To Be a (Young) Antiracist by Ibram X. Kendi and Nic Stone
I Am Not a Label: 34 disabled artists, thinkers, athletes and activists from past and present by Cerrie Burnell; illus. Lauren Baldo
Stamped: Racism, Antiracism and You by Jason Reynolds and Ibram X. Kendi (also *Stamped for Kids*)
The LGBT Purge: and the fight for equal rights in Canada by Ken Setterington
The Talk: Conversations about Race, Love & Truth by Wade Hudson and Cheryl Willis Hudson (eds.)
This Book is Anti-Racist by Tiffany Jewell; illus. Aurelia Durand (also *This Book Is Anti-Racist Journal*)
What Does Hate Look Like? by Sameea Jimenez, Corrine Promislow and Larry Swartz
Unstoppable: Women with Disabilities by Helen Wolfe; illus. Karen Patkau

Poetry

Ain't Burned all the Bright by Jason Reynolds; artwork by Jason Griffin
Say Her Name by Zetta Elliott; illus. Loveis Wise
Call Us What We Carry by Amanda Gorman (YA) (also *The Hill We Climb*)
We Rise, We Resist, We Raise Our Voices by Wade Hudson and Cheryl Willis-
   Hudson (eds.)
Woke: A young poet's guide to justice by Mahogany L Browne with Elizabeth
   Acevedo and Olivia Gatwood; illus. Theodore Taylor III

Professional Resources

References and Recommended Resources

Adesina, M. (2022). *Muric reacts to attack on mosque in Delta.* PM News.https://pmnewsnigeria.com/2022/12/03/muric-reacts-to-attack-on-mosque-in-delta/

Airton, L. (2018). *Gender: Your guide: A gender-friendly primer on what to know, what to say, and what to do in the new gender culture.* Toronto, ON: Adams Media.

Andone, D., Hanna, J., Sterling, J., & Murphy, P. P. (2018). *Hate crime charges filed in Pittsburgh synagogue shooting that left 11 dead.* CNN. https://www.cnn.com/2018/10/27/us/pittsburgh-synagogue-active-shooter/index.html

Associated Press. (2013). *Transgender teen killed by mob in Jamaica.* CBC News. https://www.cbc.ca/news/world/transgender-teen-killed-by-mob-in-jamaica-1.1366239

BBC. (2021). *Muslim family in Canada killed in 'premeditated' truck attack.* BBC News. https://www.bbc.com/news/world-us-canada-57390398

Braich, B. (2022). *Muslim community in B.C. calls for concrete action to address islamophobia.* CBCnews. https://www.cbc.ca/news/canada/british-columbia/islamophobia-in-b-c-1.6576808

Callaghan, T. D. (2018). *Homophobia in the hallways: Heterosexism and transphobia in Canadian Catholic schools.* Toronto, ON: University of Toronto Press.

Campbell, A. B. (2018). *The invisible student in the Jamaican classroom.* CreateSpace.

Campbell, A., & Watson, K. (2021). "Fostering Belonging" *Principal Connections,* 24(3), 10–11.

Campbell, I. (2022). *Northern advocates say homophobia still a present issue.* Northern Ontario. CTVNews https://northernontario.ctvnews.ca/northern-advocates-say-homophobia-still-a-present-issue-1.6179811

Coloroso, B. (2003). *The Bully, The Bullied and the Bystander.* New York, NY: HarperCollins.

____ (2012). *Just Because It's Not Wrong Doesn't Make It Right: Teaching Kids to Think and Act Ethically.* Toronto, ON: Penguin Canada.

Craig, G. (2022). Buffalo Tops shooter pleads guilty to murder, hate crime charges in mass killing. *USA Today.* https://www.usatoday.com/story/news/nation/2022/11/28/buffalo-shooter-payton-gendron-pleads-guilty/10789292002/

DiAngelo, R. (2018). *White Fragility: Why it's so hard for white people to talk about racism.* Boston, MA: Beacon Press.

Diallo, H. Cooper (2021). *#Black in School.* Regina, SK: University of Regina Press.

Diverlus, R., Hudson, S., & Ware, S. M. (2020). *Until we are free: Reflections on Black Lives Matter in Canada.* Regina, SK: University of Regina Press.

Duquette, C. (2022). *Finding a Place for Every Student; Inclusive practices, social belonging and differentiated instruction in elementary classrooms.* Markham, ON: Pembroke.

Eldridge, J. & McLafferty, D. (2021). *Hearts and Minds Matter.* http:// heartsandmindsmatter.com

Ellis, R., Fantz, A., Karimi, F., & McLaughlin, E. C. (2016). *Orlando shooting: 49 killed, shooter pledged Isis Allegiance.* CNN. https://www.cnn.com/2016/06/12/us/orlando-nightclub-shooting/index.html

Europol. (2022). *Tackling hate crime across Europe: Second joint action day targets over 170 individuals.* European Union Agency for Law Enforcement Cooperation. https://www.europol.europa.eu/media-press/newsroom/news/tackling-hate-crime-across-europe-second-joint-action-day-targets-over-170-individuals

Francisco, P., & Muggah, R. (2020). *Brazil's LGBTQ community faces surging violence, but they're fighting back.* Open Democracy. https://www.opendemocracy.net/en/democraciaabierta/violencia-anti-lgbtq-brasil-en/

Government of Canada. (2022). *Disproportionate harm: Hate crime in Canada.* Department of Justice. https://www.justice.gc.ca/eng/rp-pr/csj-sjc/crime/wd95_11-dt95_11/p2.html

Jain, S. (2022). *Hate Crimes Surge in Canada during pandemic.* Reuters. https://www.reuters.com/world/americas/hate-crimes-surge-canada-during-pandemic-2022-08-05/

Kendi, I.X. (2022). *How to Raise an Antiracist.* London, UK: One World

Liberal Party of Canada. (2022). A national action plan on combatting hate by 2022: Liberal Party of Canada. https://liberal.ca/our-platform/a-national-action-plan-on-combatting-hate-by-2022/

Love, B. (2020). *We Want to Do More Than Survive: Abolitionist teaching and the pursuit of educational freedom.* Boston, MA: Beacon Press.

Lundy, K. Gould (2019). *Stand Up and Teach.* Markham, ON: Pembroke .

_____ (2020). *Teaching Fairly in an Unfair World, 2nd edition.* Markham, ON: Pembroke.

Lundy, K. Gould & Swartz, L. (2011) *Creating Caring Classrooms.* Markham, ON: Pembroke.

Maynard, R. (2017). *Policing Black Lives: State violence in Canada from slavery to the present.* Halifax, NS: Fernwood Publishing.

Mcguirk, R. (2022). *Australian inquiry probes 40 years of gay hate killings.* City News. https://toronto.citynews.ca/2022/11/02/australian-inquiry-probes-40-years-of-gay-hate-killings/

Montpetit, J. (2023). *Quebec City Mosque shooting. The Canadian Encyclopedia.* https://www.thecanadianencyclopedia.ca/en/article/quebec-city-mosque-shooting

Moreau, G. (2022). *Police-reported crime statistics in Canada, 2021.* Statistics Canada. https://www150.statcan.gc.ca/n1/pub/85-002-x/2022001/article/00013-eng.htm

Murphy, S. (2019). *Fostering Mindfulness.* Markham, ON: Pembroke.

Oluo, I. (2019). *So you want to talk about race.* Cypress, CA: Seal Press.

Proctor, J. (2020). *The difficult history of prosecuting hate in Canada.* CBC News. https://www.cbc.ca/news/canada/british-columbia/racists-attacks-court-hate-crimes-1.5604912

Rios, E. (2022). *Hate incidents against Asian Americans continue to surge, study finds. The Guardian.* https://www.theguardian.com/us-news/2022/jul/21/asian-americans-hate-incidents-study

Rosen, K. (2022). *Communities left grieving after 4 indigenous women are believed to have been killed by serial killer.* CTV News. https://winnipeg.ctvnews.ca/communities-left-grieving-after-4-indigenous-women-are-believed-to-have-been-killed-by-serial-killer-1.6178677

Saad, L. F. (2022). *Me and White Supremacy: Combat racism, change the world, and become a good ancestor.* London, UK: Quercus Books.

Singleton, G. E., & Linton, C. (2006). *Courageous Conversations about Race: A field guide for achieving equity in schools and beyond.* Thousand Oaks, CA: Corwin Press.

Slevin, C. (2022). *Colorado LGBTQ nightclub shooting suspect charged with hate crimes.* PBS. https://www.pbs.org/newshour/nation/colorado-lgbtq-nightclub-shooting-suspect-charged-with-hate-crimes

Swan, M. (2020). *Religion a factor in one-third of hate crimes in Canada.* Grandin Media. https://grandinmedia.ca/religion-a-factor-in-one-third-of-hate-crimes-in-canada/

Swartz, L. (2020). *Teaching Tough Topics: How do I use children's literature to build a deeper understanding of social justice, equity and diversity?* Markham, ON: Pembroke.

Taylor, S. R. (2021). *The Body Is Not an Apology: The power of radical self-love.* Oakland, CA: Berrett-Koehler Publishers.

Yuill, A. (2018), *Reaching and Teaching Them All.* Markham, ON: Pembroke

Online Resources

Adichie, C. *The Danger of a Single Story* (TED TALK). https://www.ted.com/talks/chimamanda_ngozi_adichie_the_danger_of_a_single_story/c

The Canadian Anti-Hate Network. *Confronting and Preventing Hate in Canadian Schools: A Toolkit*; contact info@antihte.ca, or https://www.antihate.school/

Canadian Institute of Child Health. (2014). *The Health of Canada's Children and Youth.* https://cichprofile.ca/module/9/section/5/page/percentage-of-canadian-students-in-grades-6-through-10-who-reported-being-made-fun-of-because-of-their-body-weight-by-weight-category-and-frequency-of-bullying-canada-2014/

The Centre for Israel and Jewish Affairs (CIJA). *Unlearn It:* a resource hub for educators and parents to learn about, identify, and take action to address antisemitism. unlearnit.ca

CISA (Canadian Institute for the Study of Antisemitism). *Choose Your Voice: An online teaching resource.* https://www.voicesintoaction.ca/

CISA (Canadian Institute for the Study of Antisemitism). *Voices into Action: An online teaching resource.* https://www.voicesintoaction.ca/

Cultures of Dignity. (2019). *How to talk to Kids about Race and Racism: Parent toolkit, Cultures of Dignity* https://culturesofdignity.com/blog/guest-blogs/how-to-talk-to-kids-about-race-and-racism/

Elementary Teachers Federation of Ontario. (2021). *Stop Cyberbullying.* https://www.facebook.com/ETFOprovincialoffice/photos/a.404938019530992/4905329012825181/?type=3

Government of Canada, 2020. The health of Canadian youth: Findings from the health behaviour in school-aged children study. https://www.canada.ca/en/public-health/services/publications/science-research-data/youth-findings-health-behaviour-school-aged-children-study.html

Learning for Justice: Classroom Culture – Critical Practices for Anti-Bias Education https://www.learningforjustice.org/magazine/publications/critical-practices-for-antibias-education/classroom-culture

Powell, J. A. *Opening to the Question of Belonging* https://onbeing.org/programs/john-a-powell-opening-to-the-question-of-belonging-may2018/

_____ "Creating the Conditions for Belonging and Breathing in a Toxic Environment" https://www.youtube.com/watch?v=IpxT-8Qodnw

Recommended Articles

Baker-Bell, A. (2020). "Dismantling anti-black linguistic racism in English language arts classrooms: Toward an anti-racist black language pedagogy" *Theory Into Practice*, 59(1), 8–21.

Bemiller, M. (2019). "Inclusion for all? An exploration of Teacher's Reflections on Inclusion in Two Elementary Schools" *Journal of Applied Social Science*, 13(1), 74–88. https://doi.org/10.1177/1936724419826254

Campbell, A., & Watson, K. (2021). "Fostering Belonging" *Principal Connections*, 24(3), 10–11.

_____ (2021). "From Awareness to Action" *The Register*, 23(2), 15–21.

Campbell, A. B. (2019). "Eight 'Good Practices' for Engaging in Courageous Conversations" https://www.queensu.ca/hreo/together-we-are/eight-good-practices-engaging-courageous-conversations

Coston, E. (2017). "Anti-LGBT Hate Crimes in the US" (No. 10607041) [Dissertation, Stony Brook University]. ProQuest Dissertations Publishing. http://hdl.handle.net/11401/78328

Crouch, R., Keys, C.B., McMahon, S.D. (2014). "Student–Teacher Relationships Matter for School Inclusion: School Belonging, Disability, and School Transitions" *Journal of Prevention & Intervention in the Community*, 42:1, 20-30, DOI: 10.1080/10852352.2014.855054

Igarashi, A. (2021). "Hate Begets Hate: Anti-refugee violence increases anti-refugee attitudes in Germany" *Ethnic and Racial Studies*, 44(11), 1914–1934. https://doi.org/10.1080/01419870.2020.1802499

Kallman, J., Han, J., & Vanderbilt, D. L. (2021). "What Is Bullying?" *Clinics in Integrated Care*, 5, 100046. https://doi.org/10.1016/j.intcar.2021.100046

Kehoe, J. (2020). "Anti-LGBTQ hate: An analysis of situational variables" *Journal of Hate Studies*, 16(1), 21–34. https://doi.org/10.33972/jhs.154

Ladson-Billings, G. (2021). "Three Decades of Culturally Relevant, Responsive, & Sustaining Pedagogy: What Lies Ahead?" *The Educational Forum*, 85(4), 351–354. https://doi.org/10.1080/00131725.2021.1957632

Meyer, D. (2008). "Interpreting and experiencing anti-queer violence: Race, class, and gender differences among LGBT hate crime victims" *Race, Gender & Class*, 15(3), 262–282. https://www.jstor.org/stable/41674664

Van de Kleut, G. (2011). "The Whiteness of Literacy Practice in Ontario" *Race, Ethnicity and Education*, 14:5, 699-726, DOI.1080/13613324.2011.585338

Perspective References and Resources

Perspective by Jennifer Brant, page 34

Video Resources

Where the Sprit Lives, 1989 film
Our Sisters in Spirit (MMIWG documentary), 2016
  https://youtu.be/zdzM6krfaKY

Fiction and Nonfiction Books

Sweetgrass Basket by Marlene Carvell (YA)
Indian Horse by Richard Wagamese
The Marrow Thieves by Cherie Dimaline
Ravensong by Lee Maracle
The Break by Katherena Vermette
Seven Fallen Feathers by Tanya Talaga

Nonfiction Resources

Truth and Reconciliation in Canadian Schools, Pamela Rose Toulouse
Achieving Indigenous Student Success: A Guide for 9 to 12 Classrooms, Pamela Rose Toulouse
Residential Schools in Canada: http://education. historicacanada.ca/en/tools/261
Treaties in Canada: http://education.historicacanada.ca/ en/tools/260
Accountability in Our Lifetime: A Call to Honour the Rights of Indigenous Children and Youth. First Nations Caring Society: Senior Educational Resources. https://fncaringsociety.com/sites/default/files/ accountability_in_our_lifetime.pdf

Perspective by Lindsay Cavanaugh, page 45

The Anti-Oppression Network. *Allyship.* https:// theantioppressionnetwork.com/allyship/
Borrell, J. (2020). *International Day Against Homophobia, Transphobia and biphobia (IDAHOT) the EU is going rainbow, "Breaking the silence"* European Union: External Action https://www. eeas.europa.eu/eeas/international-day-against- homophobia-transphobia-and-biphobia-idahot-eu- going-rainbow-_en
Drescher, J. (2015). *Out of DSM: Depathologizing homosexuality.* Behavioral Sciences. https://www. ncbi.nlm.nih.gov/pmc/articles/PMC4695779/
Erasing 76 Crimes. *68 Countries Where Homosexuality is Illegal* https://76crimes. com/76countries-where-homosexuality-is-illegal/
GLAAD. (2007). *Be an ally & a friend.* https://www. glaad.org/resources/ally

Government of Ontario. (2021). *Ontario Supporting 2SLGBTQI+ Students.* Ontario Newsroom. https://news.ontario.ca/en/release/1000346/ ontario-supporting-2slgbtqi-students
Mikulec, E. A., & Miller, P. C. (2017). *Queering Classrooms: Personal narratives and educational practices to support Lgbtq youth in Schools.* Charlotte, NC: Information Age Publishing.
Rao, S. (2020). *Dwyane Wade opens up about how he and Gabrielle Union support their   child Zaya's gender identity. The Washington Post.* https://www. washingtonpost.com/arts-entertainment/2020/02/11/ dwyane-wade-opens-up-about-how-he-gabrielle- union-support-their-childs-gender-identity/
Yuen, K. (2019). *'I just ignored it': Violent, homophobic incidents common in high schools but few students report them.* CBCnews. https://www.cbc.ca/ news/canada/toronto/i-just-ignored-it-violent- homophobic-incidents-common-in-high-schools- but-few-students-report-them-1.5332784

Perspective by Kaschka Watson, page 52

Barriffe, N., DePoe, D., & William, P. (2021, April 29). *Human Rights at the TDSB: Complex but-surely-possible.* School Magazine. https:// educationactiontoronto.com/articles/human-rights- at-the-tdsb-complex-but-surely-possible/
Campbell, A. B., & Watson, K. (2021a). "From Awareness to Action: Disrupting racism/anti-Black racism as education leaders" *The Register*, 23(2), 15–21.
Campbell, A. B., & Watson, K. (2021b). "Fostering Belonging" *Principal Connections*, 24(3), 10-11.
CBC News. (2020). *Race Was a Factor in Handcuffing of 6-Year-Old Black Girl in Mississauga School, Tribunal Say*s. https://www.cbc.ca/news/canada/ toronto/human-rights-tribunal-peel-police-girl- handcuffed-1.5483456
Freeman, J., & Fox, C. (2020). "Ontario Student 'Heartbroken' After Yearbook Message Honouring Grandma Replaced With Racist Slur" *CTV News* Toronto. https://toronto.ctvnews.ca/ontario-student- heartbroken-after-yearbook -message-honouring- grandma-replaced-with-racist-slur-1.5143559
Henry, F., Dua, E., James, C. E., Kobayashi, A., Li, P., Ramos, H., & Smith, M. S. (2017). *The equity myth: Racialization and Indigeneity at Canadian universities.* Vacnouver, BC: UBC Press.

Lopez, A. E. (2013). "Embedding and Sustaining Equitable Practices in Teachers' Everyday Work: A framework for critical action" *Teaching & Learning*, 7(3), 1-15.

Maynard, R. (2022). Canadian Education Is Steeped in Anti-Black Racism. *The Walrus*. https://thewalrus.ca/canadian-education-is-steeped-in-anti-black-racism/

McMahon, B., & Portelli, J. P. (2012). *Student Engagement in Urban Schools: Beyond neoliberal discourses*. Charlotte, NC: Information Age Publishing.

Milner, H. R., & Smithey, M. (2003). "How teacher educators created a course curriculum to challenge and enhance preservice teachers' thinking and experience with diversity" *Teaching Education*, 14(3), 293–305. doi: 10.1080/1047621032000135195

Murray, K., Te, A., & Watt, J. (2020). *Addressing Anti-AsianRracism: A resource for educators*. Elementary Teachers' Federation of Ontario and Toronto District School Board. https://www.tdsb.on.ca/Portals/0/docs/Addressing%20Anti-Asian%20Racism%20Resource%20Booklet%20final%20web%20Jan%2024.pdf

Portelli, J. P. (2010). *Leadership for Equity in Education: Deficit thinking is a major challenge*. Federation for the Humanities and Social Sciences Blog. https://www.federationhss.ca/en/node/163

Schmidt, B. (2020). "Designing Schools of the Future: Unlocking student wisdom" *The Register*, 23(2), 15-21.

Shields, C., Bishop. R., & Mazawi, A. (2005). *Pathologizing Practices: The impact of deficit thinking on education*. New York, NY: Peter Lang.

Swartz, L. (2020). *Teaching Tough Topics: How do I use children's literature to build a deeper understanding of social justice, equity, and diversity?* Markham, ON: Pembroke Publishers.

Yau, M., Rosolen, L., & Archer, B. (2015a). *Census Portraits, Understanding Our Students' Backgrounds: East Asian students report* (Report No. 14/15-16). Toronto District School Board. tdsb.on.ca/Portals/research/docs/reports/ Portrait_Census2011-12_EastAsian_FINAL_report.pdf.

Perspective by Karen Mock, page 65

References

Baddiel, D. (2021). *Jews Don't Count: How identity politics failed one particular identity*. London, UK: TLS Books, HarperCollins Publishers.

Mock, Karen R. "Focus on Human Rights" column in *Canadian Social Studies*

—"Freedom of Expression vs. Political Correctness—Where Do You Draw the Line" Vol. 30, No. 1, 1995

— "Presenting 'the other side'" Vol. 30, No. 4, 1996.

— "Victims, Perpetrators, Bystanders, and Activists—Who Are They? Who are You?" Vol 31, No. 2, 1996.

_____. (1996). "Anti-Semitism in Canada Today: Realities, Remedies and Implications for Anti-Racism" in James, C. (Ed.) *Perspectives on RACiSM and the Human Services Sector: A Case for Change*. Toronto, ON: University of Toronto Press.

_____. (1996). "From Multiculturalism to Anti-Racism to Equity: Sharing Power or Grabbing Power?" McLeod, K.A. & De Koninck, Z. (Eds) in *Multicultural Education: The State of the Art National Study*. Winnipeg, MB: Canadian Association of Second Language Teachers.

_____. (2000) "Holocaust and Hope—Holocaust Education in the Context of Anti-Racist Education in Canada" in DeCoste, F.C. & Schwartz, B. (Eds). *The Holocaust's Ghost: Writings on Art, Politics, Law and Education*. Edmonton, AB: University of Alberta Press, 465–482

Related Resources

American Jewish Committee. (2021). *Translate Hate: Glossary of antisemitic terms, phrases, conspiracies, cartoons, themes, and memes*. https://www.ajc.org/sites/default/files/pdf/2021-02/AJC_Translate-Hate-Glossary-2021.pdf

Anti-Defamation League (ADL) (2022). *What Is… Antisemitism, Anti-Zionism, Anti-Israel Bias?* https://www.adl.org/resources/tools-and-strategies/what-antisemitism-anti-zionism-anti-israel-bias

Facing History & Ourselves. https://www.facinghistory.org/ (for workshops, resource materials, inclusive education)

League for Human Rights of B'nai Brith Canada, *Taking Action Against Hate: Protection, Prevention and Partnerships (A Manual for Practitioners, Educators and Community)*; also *Yom Hashoah Teachers Guide* www.bnaibrith.ca

Periphery Curriculum Workshop (organization of Jews of Color), *No Silence on Race*. www.nosilenceonrace.ca

Perspective by Steph Tuters and Sophie Stokkermans, page 99

References

Canadian Institute of Child Health. (2014). The Health of Canada's Children and Youth. https://cichprofile.ca/module/9/section/5/page/percentage-of-canadian-students-in-grades-6-through-10-who-reported-being-made-fun-of-because-of-their-body-weight-by-weight-category-and-frequency-of-bullying-canada-2014/

Elementary Teachers Federation of Ontario. (2021). *Stop Cyberbullying.* https://www.facebook.com/ETFOprovincialoffice/photos/a.404938019530992/4905329012825181/?type=3

Government of Canada (2020). *The Health of Canadian Youth: Findings from the health behaviour in school-aged children study.* https://www.canada.ca/en/public-health/services/publications/science-research-data/youth-findings-health-behaviour-school-aged-children-study.html

Resources

Dove. *Dove Self Esteem Project.* https://www.dove.com/ca/en/dove-self-esteem-project/school-workshops-on-body-image-confident-me.html

Feder, T. (2021). *Bodies Are Cool.* New York, NY: Penguin Young Readers Group.

Health Powered Kids. *Self Esteem and Body Image Lesson Planning Tool.* https://healthpoweredkids.org/lessons/self-esteem-and-body-image/

Ontario Tech University. *Teach Body Image Portal for Teacher and Parents.* http://teachbodyimage.com/

Taylor, S. (2018). *Celebrate Your Body (and it's changes, too!): The ultimate puberty book for girls.* Emeryville, CA: Rockridge Press.

Women's Health Clinic. (2018) *Resources to Support Healthy Body Image in the Classroom.* https://womenshealthclinic.org/wp-content/uploads/2018/08/Resources-to-Support-Healthy-Body-Image-Learning-in-the-Classroom-web.pdf

Perspective by Ardavan Eizadirad, page 106

Ahmed, S. (2021). *Complaint!* Durham, NC: Duke University Press.

Arao, B., & Clemens, K. (2013). "From Safe Spaces to Brave Spaces: A new way to frame dialogue around diversity and social justice" *The Art of Effective Facilitation: Reflections from Social Justice Educators.* L.M. Andreman (Ed). 135–150. Sterling, VA: Stylus Publishing.

BBC News (2020). *Black Lives Matter Founders: We fought to change history and we won.* https://www.bbc.com/news/world-us-canada-55106268

Bullying Canada. (2022). *Get Help.* https://www.bullyingcanada.ca/get-help/

Campbell, A., & Eizadirad, A. (2022). "Cultivating Brave Spaces to Take Risks to

Challenge Systemic Oppression" In Eizadirad, A., Campbell, A., & Sider, S. (Eds.). *Counternarratives of Pain and Suffering as Critical Pedagogy: Disrupting Oppression in Educational Contexts.* Milton Park, UK: Routledge.

Eizadirad, A., & Campbell, A. (2021). "Visibilizing our pain and wounds as resistance and activist pedagogy to heal and hope: Reflections of 2 racialized professors" *Diaspora, Indigenous, and Minority Education,* 1–11. Doi: 10.1080/15595692.2021.1937600

Hanna, K. B. (2019). "Pedagogies in the Flesh: Building an anti-racist decolonized classroom" *Frontiers: A Journal of Women Studies, 40*(1), 229-244.

Herrmann, J. (2017). "Brave/r Spaces vs. Safe Spaces for LGBTQ+ in the Writing Center: Theory and practice at the University of Kansas" *The Peer Review*, 1(2), 1-16.

hooks, b. (2003). *Teaching Community: A pedagogy of hope.* Milton Park, UK: Routledge.

Kapuya, T. (2019). *Safe Spaces vs. Brave Spaces.* Diversity Equity Inclusion. https://diversityequityinclusion.wordpress.com/2019/12/12/safe-spaces-vs-brave-spaces/

Kumashiro, K. (2004). *Against Common Sense: Teaching and learning toward social justice.* Milton Park, UK: Routledge.

Lauren, D. (2020). "Let's Amplify Everyone's Voice" *Rochester Business Journal*, 36(32), 19–22.

Matias, C. E. (2013). "Tears Worth Telling: Urban teaching and the possibilities of racial justice" *Multicultural Perspectives*, 15(4), 187-193.

McIntosh, P. (2003). "White Privilege: Unpacking the invisible knapsack" S. Plous (Ed.), *Understanding Prejudice and Discrimination* (191–196). New York, NY: McGraw-Hill.

National Equity Project. (2022). *Lens of Systemic Oppression.* https://www.nationalequityproject.org/frameworks/lens-of-systemic-oppression

Ng, W. (2004). *A Tool for Everyone: Revelations from the "Power Flower"* LGBTQ2S Toolkit. http://lgbtq2stoolkit.learningcommunity.ca/wp/wp-content/uploads/2014/12/flower-power-exercise.pdf

Randa, R., Reyns, B. W., & Nobles, M. R. (2016). "Measuring the Effects of Limited and Persistent School Bullying Victimization: Repeat victimization, fear, and adaptive behaviors" *Journal of Interpersonal Violence, 34*(2), 392–415. https://doi.org/10.1177/0886260516641279

Sevelius, J. M., Gutierrez-Mock, L., Zamudio-Haas, S., McCree, B., Ngo, A., Jackson, A., Clynes, C.,

Venegas, L., Salinas, A., Herrera, C., Stein, E., Operario, D., & Gamarel, K. (2020). "Research with Marginalized Communities: Challenges to continuity during the COVID-19 pandemic *AIDS and Behavior, 24*(7), 2009–2012. https://doi.org/10.1007/s10461-020-02920-3

Index